# THE ULTIMATE BEGINNER SERIES
# DRUMS COMPLETE

**Sandy Gennaro • Tom Brechtlein • Mike Finkelstein • Joe Testa**

Alfred Publishing Co., Inc.
16320 Roscoe Blvd., Suite 100
P.O. Box 10003
Van Nuys, CA 91410-0003
**alfred.com**

Book and DVD (with case)
ISBN-10: 0-7390-5620-4
ISBN-13: 978-0-7390-5620-2

Book and DVD (without case)
ISBN-10: 0-7390-5621-2
ISBN-13: 978-0-7390-5621-9

Cover photographs:
Blue energy © istockphoto.com/Raycat
Drums courtesy of Mapex

# CONTENTS

# BLUES DRUMS

**CONTENTS**

# CONTENTS

## ROCK DRUMS

# INTRODUCTION

No matter what style you play, the drummer's role is to be the heartbeat and the foundation of the music. Similar to learning how to ride a bike, once you learn the basic fundamentals, you never forget them. This book will give you the vocabulary necessary to allow you to grow to any level you would like to achieve. The book starts off with the basics and gradually gets you playing the blues and rock. The companion DVD will show you all the examples and songs to make learning fast and easy.

The Basics section will get you started by learning about the drum set, how to hold the sticks, how to play beats, the drummer's role in the band and much more. You'll also learn about song structure, note values and get to play fills and exercises.

The Blues section teaches you the basics of playing the blues. Topics include shuffle patterns, bass drum variations, blues Rhumba, the open hi-hat sound, fill ideas to name a few. There are also practice tips and lessons on how to develop the blues groove with a bass player.

The Rock section gives you everything you need to play great rock beats and fills. You will explore ballads, shuffles, basic rock patterns, and lots of rock fills. There are plenty of play-along tunes too.

Let's dig in and get started playing the drums.

The included DVD contains MP3 audio files of every example in the book. Use the MP3s to ensure you're capturing the feel of the examples and interpreting the rhythms correctly.

To access the MP3s on the DVD, place the DVD in your computer's DVD-ROM drive. In Windows, double-click on My Computer, then right-click on the DVD drive icon. Select Explore, then double-click on the DVD-ROM Materials folder. For Mac, double-click on the DVD icon on your desktop, then double-click on the DVD-ROM Materials folder.

# BASIC DRUMS

# THE BASS DRUM

***Range:*** The drum set contains a wide range of sounds. To build from the bottom (low range) to the top (high range) we start with the bass drum. In most music, the bass drum locks in with what the bass guitar is playing.

***Explanation and Position:*** The bass drum is played with a bass drum pedal which is operated by the foot. Position your seat height so your thighs are parallel to the floor. The front of the drum may be slightly elevated to allow better sound projection.

***How to Play:*** There are two basic techniques for playing the bass drum:

1) Heel Down: Your foot remains flat on the foot pedal. Power and control come from the ankle. Use the same action as tapping your foot on the ground.

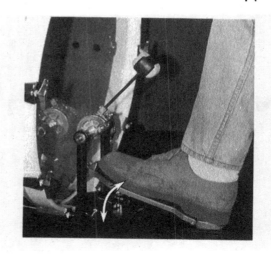 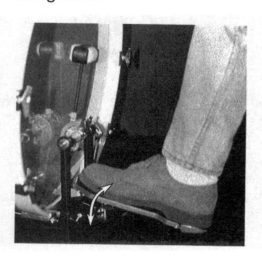

2) Heel Up: The ball of your foot is placed on the widest part of the pedal. The entire leg is used in conjunction with the toes to achieve better control and power.

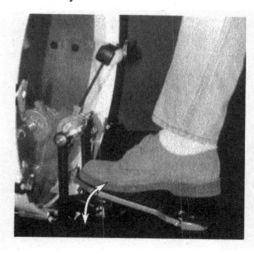 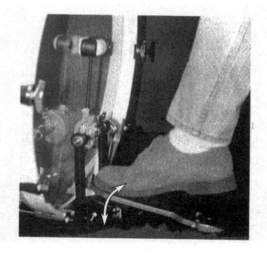

How well you play is based on how relaxed you are. Being relaxed means being comfortable. You should experiment to find what is best for you.

# Lesson 1

a) Listen to the music without the bass drum.

b) Now listen to the music with the bass drum. Listen to what the bass drum adds to the music.

c) Begin by counting: 1 & 2 & 3 & 4 &

d) Count and play the circled numbers with right foot on the bass drum.

        ①   &   ②   &   ③   &   ④   &

On our drum graph, it would look like this:

e) Now count and play with the music.

# THE SNARE DRUM

**Range:** The snare drum sound is the mid range of the set. It differs from the rest of the drums because there are wire snares that rest against the bottom head. When the top head is played, air is forced through the drum causing the bottom head and the wire snares to vibrate. This creates the snare drum's unique sound.

**Grip:** There are two types of grips:

1) Matched Grip: Both hands are held in the same way. Grip the stick between the second knuckle of the index finger and thumb one-third of the way up from the butt end. This prevents the stick from sliding and gives you control. The remaining fingers wrap lightly around the stick. The wrist and fingers should be in line with the forearm so that the stick becomes a natural extension of the arm.

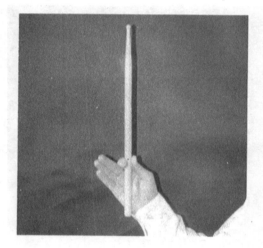 

2) Traditional Grip: The right hand holds the stick in the matched grip style. The left hand, however, is held in a completely different way. The stick is held in the webbing of the hand between the thumb and index finger, approximately 1/3 of the distance from the butt end. The ring finger and pinky are under the stick, while the middle and index finger are on top of the stick.

 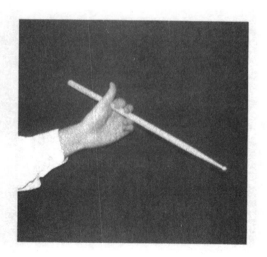

**Explanation and Position:** The position of the drum depends on the type of grip used by the player. No matter what grip you use, your stroke should be the same. The drum should be placed between your legs, not too high or low. Be careful not to position the drum so that your hand hits your thigh. When using matched grip, the drum should be flat or slightly tilted downward toward the player. With the traditional grip, the drum may be slightly tilted downward to the right.

**How to Play:** The stroke for the right hand is very similar to casting a fishing rod or cracking a whip. Strike the drum with the tip of the stick a little off center.

The rebound should be quick as if the drum were a hot stove and the stick was your hand. The idea is to get the stick off the drum as quickly as possible. This will allow the head to vibrate fully and produce the best sound.

Practice counting and playing the circled numbers. Alternate right (R.H.) and left (L.H.) hands.

      ①    &    ②    &    ③    &    ④    &
      R         L         R         L

Rim Shot: Another stroke used very often is the rim shot. A rim shot is created when the stick strikes the rim of the drum and the head of the drum at the same time.

# Lesson 2

a) Listen to the music with the bass drum and no snare drum.

b) Now listen to the music with the bass drum and snare drum. Listen to what the snare drum adds to the music.

c) Begin by counting: 1 & 2 & 3 & 4 &

The snare drum is played on the 2 and 4. This is known as the backbeat.

d) Count and play the circled numbers with your left hand.

      1    &    ②    &    3    &    ④    &
                  L                  L

e) Now count and play this snare and bass drum pattern.

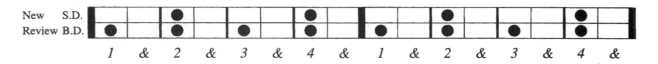

f) Play Lesson 2 with music.

# THE CYMBALS
# (HI-HAT, RIDE AND CRASH)

**Range:** The high end sounds of the drum set are produced by the cymbals.

## Hi-Hat Cymbals

**Explanation and Position:** The hi-hat consists of two cymbals that are mounted on the hi-hat stand.

The hi-hat stand contains a rod which goes through the hollow stand. It connects with the foot pedal. (The foot movement on the pedal dictates the up and down movement of the rod.)

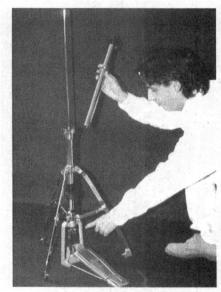

The bottom cymbal is placed upside down on the felt pad of the stand.

The top cymbal is attached to the rod with a clutch which you tighten with a wing nut. The cymbals should be 3/4" or an inch apart. When the foot pedal is pressed, the cymbals come together to make a "chick" sound.

The hi-hat should be positioned just left of the snare drum. Not too high or low, and not too forward or back.

***How to Play:*** There are two ways to play the hi-hat cymbals: with your foot or hands.

1) Hi-Hat with Foot: There are two basic techniques for playing the hi-hat with your foot.

a. Heel Down: Your foot remains flat on the foot pedal. Power and control come from the ankle.

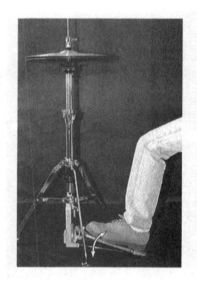

b. Heel Up: The ball of your foot is placed on the widest part of the pedal. The entire leg is used in conjunction with the toes to achieve better control and power.

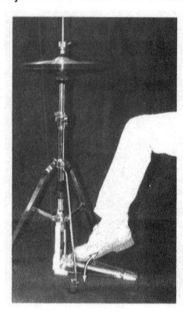

# Lesson 3

a) Listen to the music with the bass drum and snare drum.

b) Now listen to the music with the hi-hat added. Listen to what the hi-hat adds to the music.

c) Begin by counting: 1 & 2 & 3 & 4 &

d) Count and play the circled numbers with left foot on the hi-hat. (Practice both the heel up and heel down technique):

1    &    ②    &    3    &    ④    &

e) Now count and play the new hi-hat pattern with the snare and bass drum pattern. Note: The hi-hat is indicated on the drum graph with an "X" in its assigned box. Also practice playing the hi-hat on all four beats.

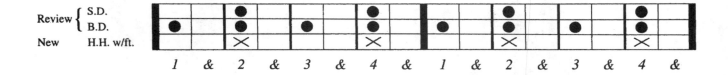

f) Play Lesson 3 with music.

2) Hi-Hat Played with the Stick: A common approach to playing the hi-hat is to keep the cymbals closed with the left foot while playing with a stick (right hand).

# Lesson 4

a) Listen to the music with the bass drum and snare drum.

b) Now listen to the music with the new hi-hat pattern added. Listen to what the new hi-hat pattern adds to the music.

c) Begin by counting: 1 & 2 & 3 & 4 &

d) Count and play the circled numbers with the right hand on the hi-hat.

①　&　②　&　③　&　④　&

e) Now count and play the new hi-hat pattern with the snare and bass drum pattern. You will have to cross the right hand over the left hand.

Note: When the hi-hat is played with the stick, it will be indicated with a "X" on its assigned *line*.

## Beat #1

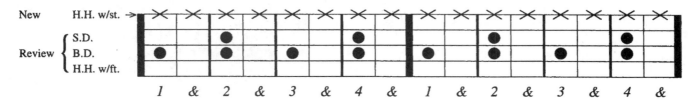

f) Play Lesson 4 with music.

# *Ride Cymbal*

***Explanation and Position:*** The ride cymbal helps change the characteristic of the beat by bringing a brighter sound to the overall mix of the drum set. More often than not it is located to the right of the bass drum.

***How To Play:*** There are many ways to play the ride cymbal. Each creates a different sound.

1) Play the cymbal with the tip of the stick 1/3 of the way in from the edge. This will produce a "ping" sound.

2) Play the cymbal with the shaft of the stick near the edge of the cymbal. This creates a broader sound.

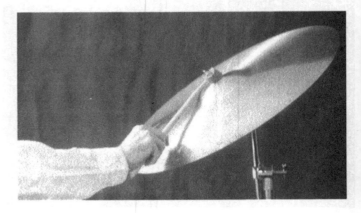

3) Play with the shaft of the stick on the bell to create an accented "ping".

# Lesson 5

a) Listen to the music with the bass drum, snare drum and hi-hat (left foot).

b) Now listen to the music with the new ride pattern added. Listen to what the new ride pattern adds to the music.

c) Begin by counting: 1 & 2 & 3 & 4 &

d) Count and play the circled numbers with right hand on the ride cymbal.

① & ② & ③ & ④ &

e) Now count and play the new ride pattern with the snare and bass drum pattern. We'll also add the hi-hat pattern learned in Lesson 3. Note: The ride cymbal is indicated on the drum graph with an "X" in its assigned box.

## Beat #2

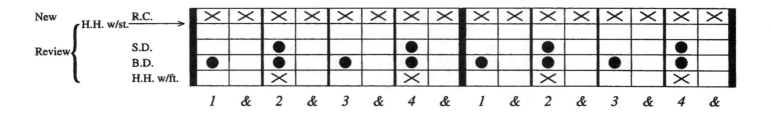

f) Play Lesson 5 with music.

# Crash Cymbal

**Explanation and Position:** One way to add excitement and high end to any given beat is to use crash cymbals. Like all cymbals, they come in different thickness and sizes to produce various tones. Their primary use is to emphasize and/or accent a certain musical phrase or idea. It is common to place a crash cymbal to the left of the bass drum.

**How To Play:** Crash cymbals are played with a "sweeping" stroke with the shaft of the stick.

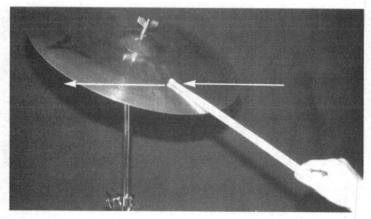

# Lesson 6

a) Listen to the music with the bass drum, snare drum and hi-hat (right hand).

b) Now listen to the music with the crash cymbal added on beat 1. Listen to what the crash cymbal adds to the music.

c) Begin by counting: 1 & 2 & 3 & 4 &

d) Count and play the circled numbers with the right hand on the crash cymbal.

       ①   &   2   &   3   &   4   &

e) Now count and play adding the crash cymbal to BEAT #1. Note: The crash cymbal is indicated on the drum graph with a "X" on its assigned *line*. We'll call this BEAT #3.

## Beat #3

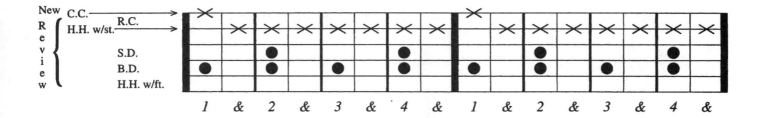

# Lesson 7 *(a variation on Lesson 6)*

We can also add the crash cymbal on 1 of BEAT #2. We'll call this BEAT #4.

## Beat #4

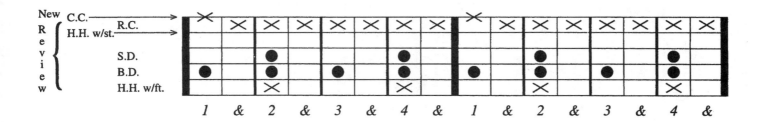

Play Lesson 7 with music.

# *Lesson 8*

## PUTTING ALL FOUR BEATS TOGETHER:

We've added a bit of music to play along with. The object of this exercise is to play each beat *four* times and immediately go on to the next one.

First listen to the example. Listen to how the beat works with the music.

Now practice each beat in succession like the example.

# Beat #1

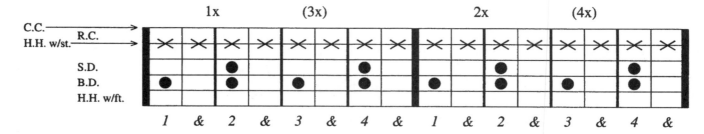

# Beat #3

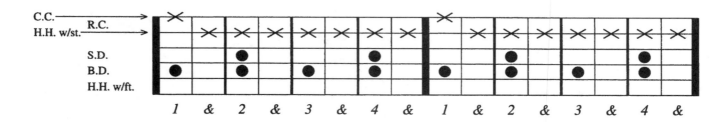

# Beat #2

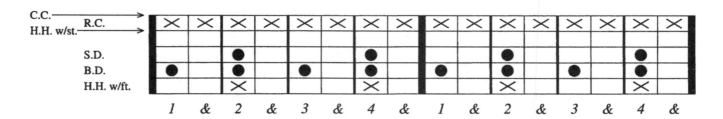

# Beat #4

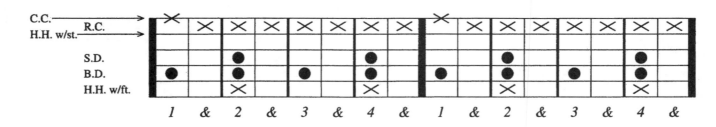

# *TEMPO*

You can play any beat at different speeds. These different speeds are called tempos. Different tempos give the beat a whole new feel and it can change the characteristic of the beat.

While practicing each tempo, concentrate on keeping steady time. Play Lesson 8 (page 20) at the new *slower* tempo.

Now play Lesson 8 at the *medium* tempo.

Play at the *fast* tempo.

# *DYNAMICS*

You can play any beat at different volumes. These different volumes are called dynamics. Different dynamics create excitement within the music and it can bring new life to a simple beat.

Now take Lesson 8 and practice each dynamic. Be careful not to slow down when you play quietly or speed up when you play loudly.

Play at the *quiet* dynamic.

Play at the *medium* dynamic.

Play at the *loud* dynamic.

# Lesson 9

Here are eight beat variations to practice. The hi-hat (R.H.) and the snare drum (L.H.) remain constant while the bass drum changes. Play each exercise along with the audio track. The first two times you play along with the beat, the second two times with just a click track. After you master each variation, practice each beat on your own with a click (metronome and/or drum machine). Remember to practice each beat at various tempos and dynamics.

1)

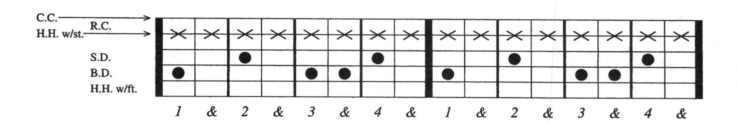

2)

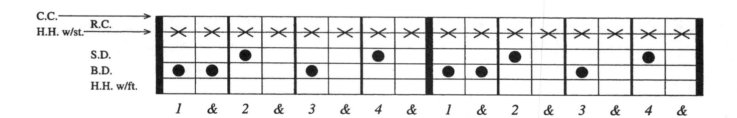

3)

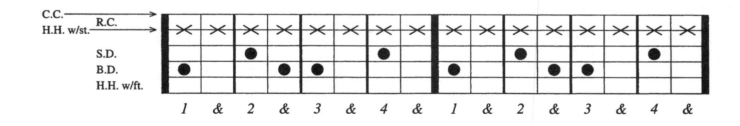

**4)**

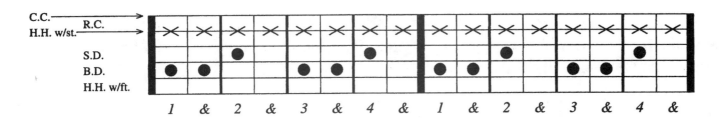

**5)**

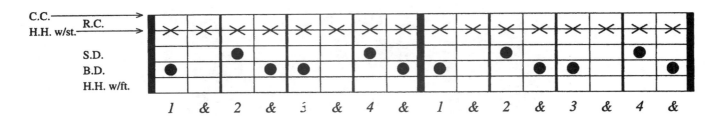

**6)**

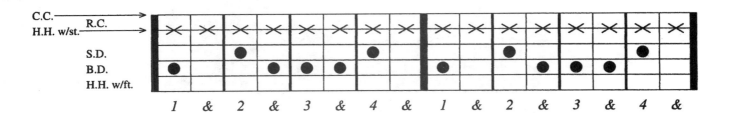

**7)**

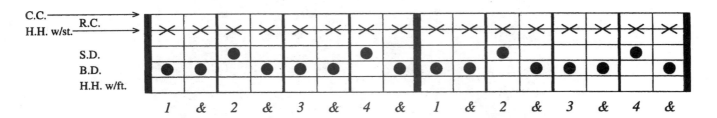

**8)**

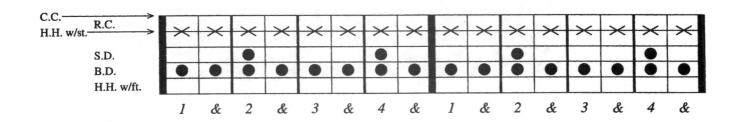

# THE TOM TOMS

**Range:** Tom toms are predominately used for fills, so their range varies from high to low. There are two types of tom toms:

**Explanation and Position:**

1) Rack Toms: These toms are mounted on top of the bass drum or on a stand that hangs over the bass drum. They are usually set up from high pitch to low pitch, left to right, the smaller toms being the higher pitched and the larger toms being the lower pitched.

2) Floor Tom: This is the biggest tom tom. It is set up to the right of the snare drum and can stand on legs or hang from a mounted stand.

Listen to the tom toms, starting high to low and back again.

Note: Regarding all the examples in Lessons 10 – 12, listen to the beat on the audio track. Immediately following the beat, you will hear just a click so that you can practice the beat on your own.

# Lesson 10

Now play BEAT #2 and add (with your left hand) the new high tom and snare patterns. We'll call this BEAT #5.

## Beat #5

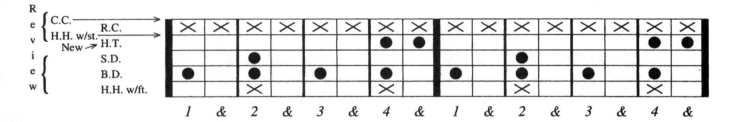

# Lesson 11

Now play BEAT #5 and play the new pattern on the floor tom instead of the high tom. This is BEAT #6.

## Beat #6

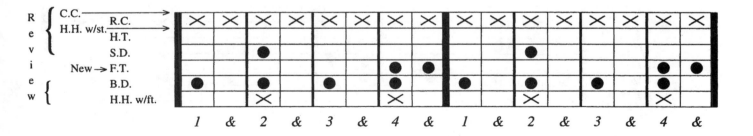

# Lesson 12

Now play BEAT #6 and play the new pattern on the floor tom, but this time play the snare pattern on the high tom. This is BEAT #7.

## Beat #7

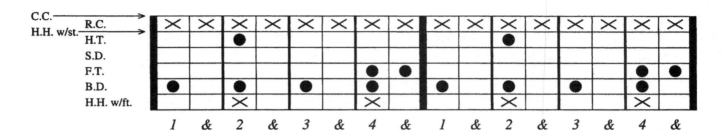

Practice BEATS #5, #6 and #7 with the ride pattern on the hi-hat.

## Beat #5 with H.H.

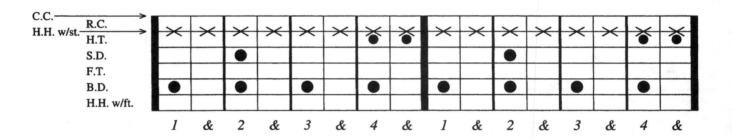

## Beat #6 with H.H.

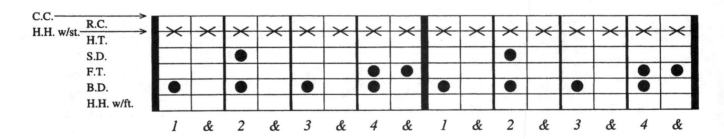

## Beat #7 with H.H.

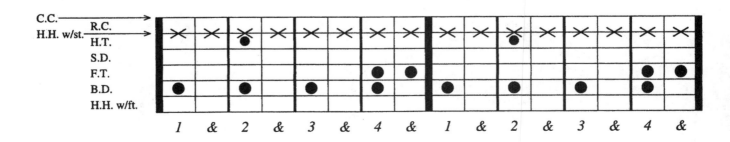

# THE E's & THE A's:
# A NEW WAY TO COUNT

## Lesson 13

a) Play the following on the snare drum with just your right hand.

```
1   &   2   &   3   &   4   &
R   R   R   R   R   R   R   R
```

b) Play in between each right hand with your left hand (L). We will call all the "L's" the "e's" and the "a's".

```
1 (e) & (a)   2 (e) & (a)   3 (e) & (a)   4 (e) & (a)
R (L) R (L)   R (L) R (L)   R (L) R (L)   R (L) R (L)
```

c) Practice this same pattern on the hi-hat.

d) " ⫽ " is called a repeat sign. When you see a repeat sign, repeat the pattern you just played.

e) Practice this pattern on the hi-hat with alternating strokes, but play every 2 and 4 on the snare drum with the right hand.

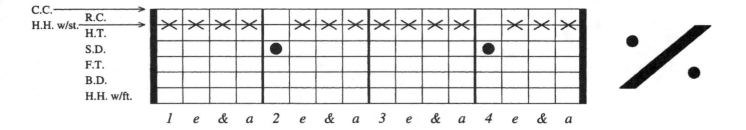

f) Now add the bass drum on the 1, 2, 3 and 4. We will call this BEAT #8. Once again, listen to the example and then play with the click.

## Beat #8

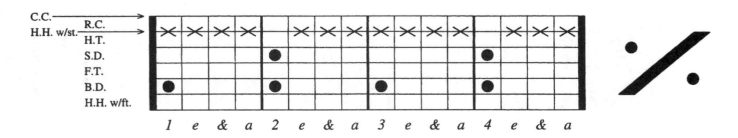

## Lesson 14

You can practice different variations based on this groove. Here are two to listen to and then practice.

1)

### Beat #9

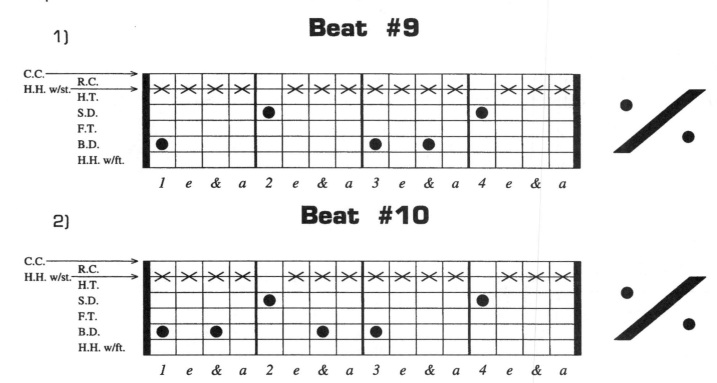

2)

### Beat #10

# THE "TRIP" AND THE "LETS": ANOTHER RHYTHM

## Lesson 15

a) Begin counting: 1 - Trip - Let - 2 - Trip - Let - 3 - Trip - Let - 4 - Trip - Let

b) To·get a feel for it, play with alternating sticking on the snare drum only.

| 1 Trip Let | 2 Trip Let | 3 Trip Let | 4 Trip Let |
|---|---|---|---|
| R **L** R | **L** R **L** | R **L** R | **L** R **L** |

c) Practice this same pattern on the hi-hat with just the right hand.

d) Now practice the right hand pattern on the hi-hat, but play every 2 and 4 on the snare drum with the left hand.

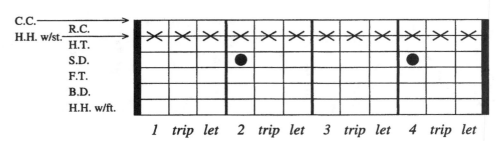

e) Now add the bass drum on beats 1, 2, 3 and 4. We will call this BEAT #11. Listen to it and then practice with the click.

## Beat #11

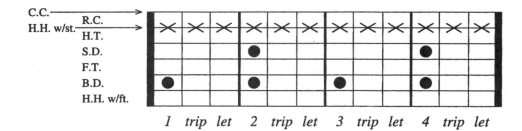 

## Lesson 16

You can practice different variations based on this groove. Here are two:

1)

## Beat #12

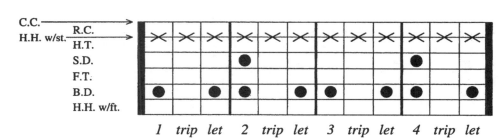 

2)

## Beat #13

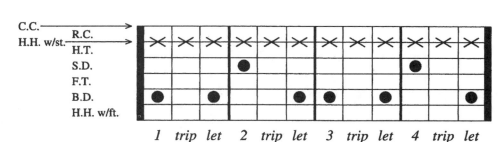 

# INTRODUCING NOTE VALUES (READING.... WHY?)

## Lesson 17

Learning how to read expands your options in learning drum fills and beats. It also allows you to communicate with other instrumentalists and to become more creative.

At this point you already know how each drum relates to the musical staff. Look how the drum graph has prepared you to read music. It is perfectly related to the musical staff:

## Drums

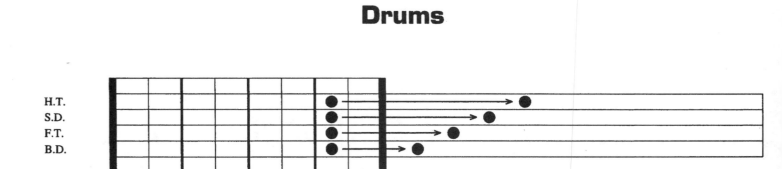

## Cymbals

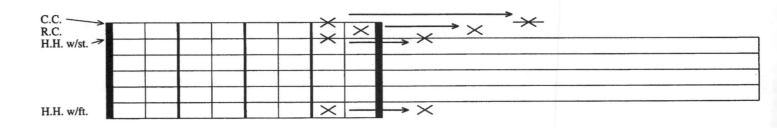

# COUNTING NOTE VALUES AND RHYTHM

## Lesson 18

Now that you understand how the drum graph relates to the musical staff, it is also important to know how the music is written on the staff. Without realizing it, you have already been reading basic notes and rhythms.

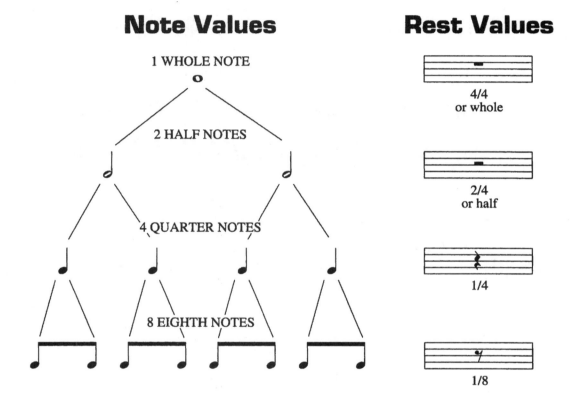

Since Lesson 1 you have been counting 1 & 2 & 3 & 4 &. The 1, 2, 3 and 4 are quarter notes and the "&'s" are eighth notes.

Eighth Notes can be divided into sixteenth notes.

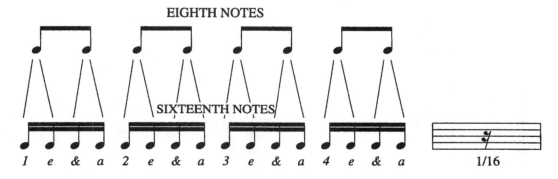

Notice you've been counting the "e's" and the "a's" since Lesson 13.

In Lesson 15 you learned what "Triplets" feel like. There are three eighth note triplets per one quarter note.

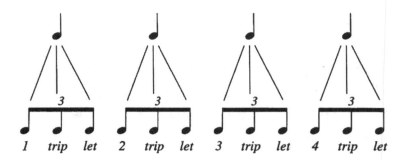

1  trip  let    2  trip  let    3  trip  let    4  trip  let

Notice the "1" "Trip" "Let" "2" "Trip" "Let" "3" "Trip" "Let" "4" "Trip" "Let" from Lesson 15.

# MEASURES, BARLINES AND TIME SIGNATURES

## Lesson 19

Music is divided into equal parts called measures. Barlines indicate the beginning and end of measures. A double barline, one thin and one thick, show the end of a piece.

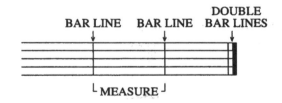

Time Signatures are placed at the beginning of a piece of music to show the number of beats (or counts) in each measure and the kind of note that receives one beat.

4 = four beats per measure
4 = quarter note gets one beat

Let's take a look at BEAT #1 and see how the drum graph translates into a bar of 4/4 in music notation.

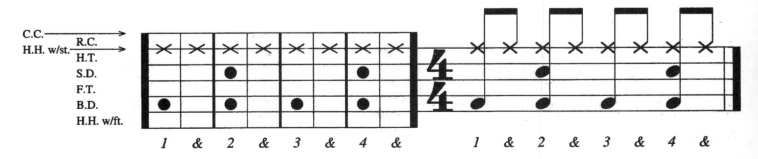

# SONG FORM

## Lesson 20

The primary function of a drummer is to play consistent time, but it is also important to support the form of the song. A basic song usually consists of three major sections: a VERSE, CHORUS and BRIDGE. There are many ways the drummer can support the song form. You can play different dynamics, variations of beats, or add drum fills.

**Drum Fills:** Drum fills are often used to lead the song from one section to the next. Listen to each example and how it sets up the musical change. Then play with the music on your own with only a click.

## 1-Beat Fills

1)

2)

3)

**4)**

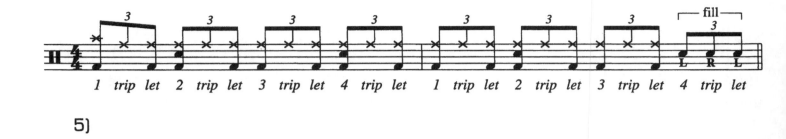

*1 trip let 2 trip let 3 trip let 4 trip let 1 trip let 2 trip let 3 trip let 4 trip let*

**5)**

*1 trip let 2 trip let 3 trip let 4 trip let 1 trip let 2 trip let 3 trip let 4 trip let*

## 2-Beat Fills

**6)**

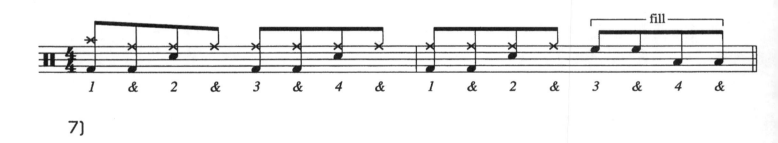

*1 & 2 & 3 & 4 & 1 & 2 & 3 & 4 &*

**7)**

*1 & 2 & 3 & 4 & 1 & 2 & 3 & 4 e & a*

**8)**

1 e & a 2 e & a 3 e & a 4 e & a   1 e & a 2 e & a 3 e & a 4 e & a

**9)**

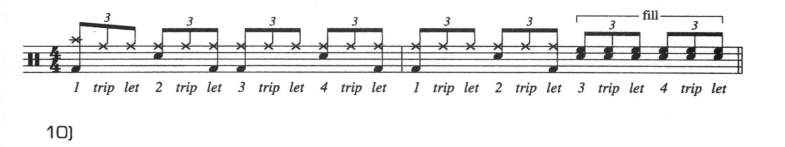

1 trip let 2 trip let 3 trip let 4 trip let   1 trip let 2 trip let 3 trip let 4 trip let

**10)**

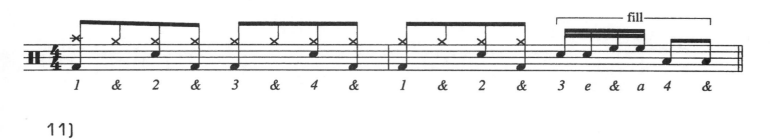

1 & 2 & 3 & 4 & 1 & 2 & 3 e & a 4 &

**11)**

1 e & a 2 e & a 3 e & a 4 e & a   1 e & a 2 e & a 3 e & a 4 e & a

**12)**

1 trip let 2 trip let 3 trip let 4 trip let   1 trip let 2 trip let 3 trip let 4 trip let

# PUTTING IT ALL TOGETHER

Now it's time for you to put all that you have learned to use. Play along with these next two songs. The first is in a rock style, the second is a 12-bar blues. The audio track will have two versions of each song, one with an example of the drum part and the other with a click so you can play along on your own.

## ROCK PLAY ALONG

*Intro:*

*Verse 1:*

*Verse 2:*

*Chorus 1:*

*Verse 3:*

*Chorus 2:*

*Bridge:*

*Gtr. Solo:*

*Chorus 3:*

*Chorus 4:*

# 12-BAR BLUES PLAY ALONG

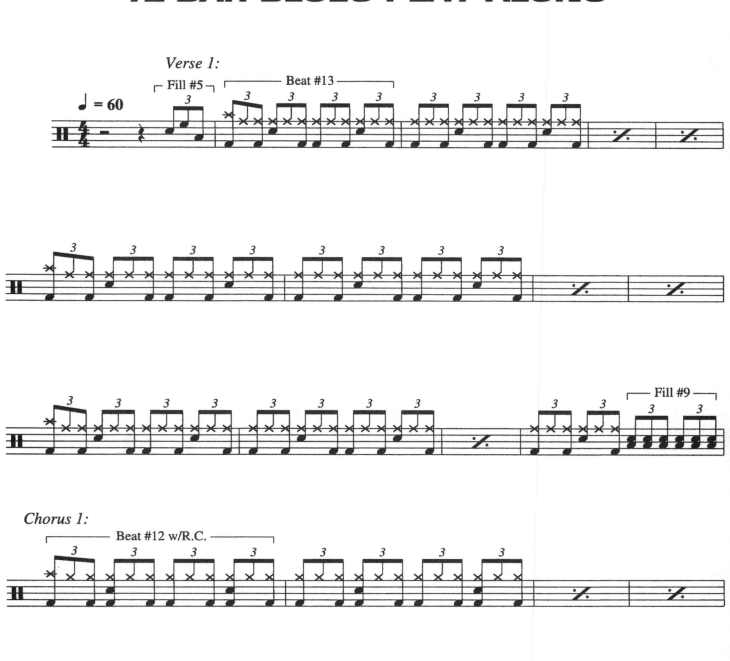

*Verse 1:*

*Chorus 1:*

*Solo 1 (Verse 2):*

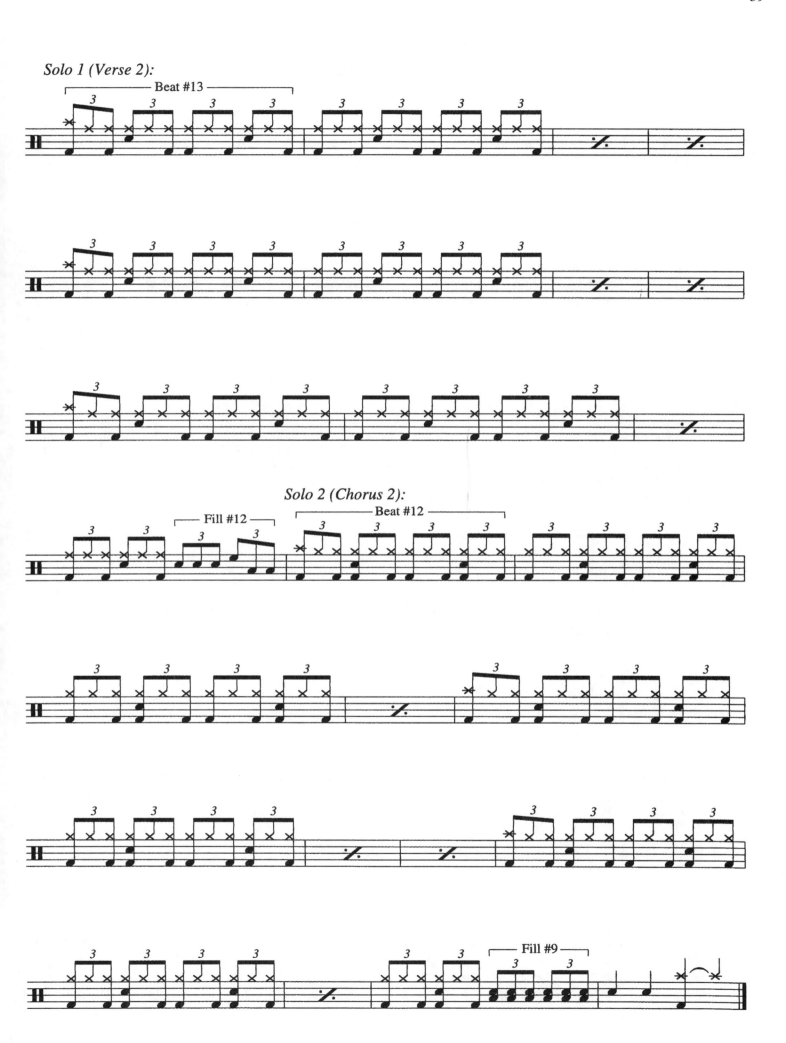

*Solo 2 (Chorus 2):*

# HAND WARM-UPS

Now that you know how to play the drums, here are some helpful exercises that will warm you up before playing. It is suggested that you practice all the warm-ups while playing the hi-hat on beats 2 and 4, and then on all 4 beats.

1)

2)

3)

4)

5)

**6)**

**7)**

**8)**

**9)**

**10)**

# BLUES DRUMS

# NOTATION KEY

| BASS DRUM | SNARE DRUM | RIM SHOT | CROSSTICK (RIM CLICK) | TOM 1 | TOM 2 | TOM 3 |
|-----------|------------|----------|-----------------------|-------|-------|-------|

| HI-HAT CLOSED W/STICK | HI-HAT HALF OPEN (SPASHY HAT) | HI-HAT OPEN | HI-HAT CLOSED | HI-HAT W/FOOT | RIDE | RIDE BELL | CRASH |
|-----------------------|-------------------------------|-------------|---------------|---------------|------|-----------|-------|

# PRACTICE TIPS

The key to practicing, performing and just plain playing well is RELAXATION! The more relaxed you are the better your mind and body can perform.

1) The first step to relaxing is stretching. You should always stretch before and after you play. By doing this you will help relax the muscles, so no unnecessary or sudden strain occurs.

2) Make sure the instruments in your drum set are set up in the most comfortable place for you. What may be comfortable for your favorite drummer or friend may not be the best for you. Every cymbal and drum should be setup so that it is very easy to play. If you notice yourself straining to play a cymbal or drum, you are probably wasting energy because of a poor setup. Playing the drums is a very physical activity and should be approached like an athlete would approach their sport.

3) Patience is a must. When practicing something new, take your time and slowly build it up. Don't go on to the next step until you feel you've mastered the first. If you're still having trouble after slowing it down, then chances are you've missed something in the previous lesson. Go back and review the lesson or exercises before.

4) Using a time keeping device, such as a metronome or drum machine, work on each exercise slowly until it is correct. If certain places are giving you more trouble than others, work on them individually one limb at a time. As you become comfortable, add the next limb and proceed until all limbs are playing with ease. Don't increase the tempo until you can play the new groove with confidence at a moderate tempo. Always make sure you stop before changing tempo. This will avoid creating the bad habit of rushing. *A drummer's primary responsibility is to lay down a steady groove. The ability to play with consistent time is something you need to strive for.*

5) Record every time you play: practices, gigs, jam sessions, etc. Then spend time listening back to yourself. Also, listen to other musicians and to all types of music as much as possible. You should spend as much time listening as you do playing.

6) Play along with all your favorite recordings. This will help you learn your favorite drummer's style, licks and musical approach. If blues is your favorite music, then play along with your favorite blues musicians (Muddy Waters, Howlin Wolf, Stevie Ray Vaughn, Robben Ford, B.B. King, John Lee Hooker, Buddy Guy, Paul Butterfield, etc). This will help you acquire that special feel that makes blues drumming unique.

7) Play with many musicians in many musical styles. You picked up this book because you're interested in blues drumming, but you shouldn't underestimate the assets of other musical styles and how they can improve your overall performance.

8) Drums are a very dynamic instrument and volume can be a major factor in your playing. It is very important to protect your ears when playing. Using earplugs can extend the life of your hearing and protect you from suffering from hearing loss or damage.

# RHYTHM NOTATION, TIME SIGNATURE & REPEATS

At the beginning of every song is a time signature. 4/4 is the most common time signature:

4 = FOUR COUNTS TO A MEASURE
4 = A QUARTER NOTE RECEIVES ONE COUNT

The top number tells you how many counts per measure.
The bottom number tells you which kind of note receives one count.

The time value of a note is determined by three things:

1) Note Head: o    •    2) Stem: ♩ ♩    3) Flag: ♪ ♪

o    This is a whole note. The note head is open and has no stem. In 4/4 time it receives 4 counts.

♩    This is a half note. It has an open note head and a stem. In 4/4 time it receives 2 counts.

♩    This is a quarter note. It has a solid note head and a stem. In 4/4 time it receives 1 count.

♪    This is an eighth note. It has a solid note head and a stem with a flag attached. In 4/4 time it receives 1/2 count.

♪    This is a sixteenth note. It has a solid note head and a stem with a double flag attached. In 4/4 time it receives 1/4 count.

♪♪♪    One count in 4/4 time can also be divided into three equal notes called eighth note triplets. To distinguish them from regular eighth notes, a small 3 appears above them. In 4/4 time one eighth note triplet receives 1/3 count.

A rest is a period of silence. Each type of note has a corresponding rest:

Whole Rest: ▬ = o = 4 counts          Half Rest: ▬ = ♩ = 2 counts

Quarter Rest: 𝄽 = ♩ = 1 count          Eighth Rest: 𝄾 = ♪ = 1/2 count

Sixteenth Rest: 𝄿 = ♪ = 1/4 count    Triplet Eighth Rest: ♪𝄾♩ = ♪♪♩ = 1/3 count

Music is divided into equal parts called measures. Barlines indicate the beginning and end of measures. A double barline (one thin and one thick) indicates the end of a piece.

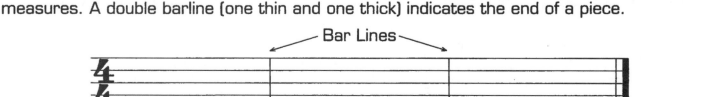

Bar Lines

Measure          Measure          Measure

The following is a chart of notes and their equal rests in 4/4 time:

 is called a repeat sign. When you see this sign, repeat the measure you just played:

Repeat signs :‖ tell us to play a section of music again. One backwards facing repeat sign means you should repeat to the beginning:

*Repeat back to the beginning.*

When a section of music falls between two repeat signs, repeat that section:

*Repeat only the section in between the repeat signs.*

*Take the repeat once, then continue on to the next section.*

Sometimes a section of music is repeated, but the ending is different the second time:

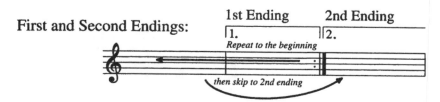

# THE BASIC SHUFFLE PATTERN

## *Lesson 21*

a) 2 bars of TRIPLET FEEL.

b) 2 bars of SHUFFLE PATTERN.

c) 4 bars of PATTERN 1 SET-UP A.

d) 4 bars of PATTERN 1 SET-UP B.

e) 4 bars of PATTERN 1 SET-UP C.

f) 4 bars of PATTERN 1.

g) 4 bars of VARIATION 1A.

h) 4 bars of VARIATION 1B.

a) **TRIPLET FEEL:** The shuffle is based on the triplet note value. A basic triplet pattern looks like this:

b) **SHUFFLE PATTERN:** To create a shuffle feel, remove all the middle triplets. Practice this with just your left hand on the snare drum. This is where the shuffle gets its swing!

c) **PATTERN 1 SET-UP A:** Play the left hand SHUFFLE PATTERN while playing quarter notes on the ride cymbal. **Note:** When learning new patterns, it is important to line up the limbs on common beats.

d) **PATTERN 1 SET-UP B:** Now add the bass drum. Notice that the bass drum pattern is the same as the ride cymbal.

e) **PATTERN 1 SET-UP C:** Now add the left foot hi-hat in unison with the bass drum and ride cymbal.

f) **PATTERN 1:** Accent (>) the snare on beats 2 and 4 with a rim shot. A rim shot is created when the stick strikes the rim of the drum at the same time as the head. The symbol for a rim shot is "⊗" in the snare drum space. This is the basic shuffle pattern.

g) **VARIATION 1A:** Play PATTERN 1 and add a crash cymbal on beat 1 of every two measures.

h) **VARIATION 1B:** Now play VARIATION 1A with the right hand on the hi-hat. In this pattern, the left foot hi-hat is not played.

# Lesson 22

a) 4 bars of PATTERN 2 SET-UP A.

b) 4 bars of PATTERN 2 SET-UP B.

c) 4 bars of PATTERN 2 SET-UP C.

d) 4 bars of PATTERN 2 SET-UP D.

e) 4 bars of PATTERN 2.

f) 4 bars of VARIATION 2A.

g) 4 bars of VARIATION 2B.

a) **PATTERN 2 SET-UP A:** Play this new ride cymbal pattern. This is known as the jazz cymbal pattern.

b) **PATTERN 2 SET-UP B:** Add the bass drum on all quarter notes.

c) **PATTERN 2 SET-UP C:** Now add the shuffle pattern on the snare drum.

d) **PATTERN 2 SET-UP D:** Add the left foot hi-hat in unison with the bass drum.

e) **PATTERN 2:** Accent (>) the snare on beats 2 and 4 with a rim shot.

f) **VARIATION 2A:** Play PATTERN 2 and add a crash cymbal on beat 1 of every two measures.

g) **VARIATION 2B:** Now play VARIATION 2A with the right hand on the hi-hat. In this pattern the left foot hi-hat is not played.

# Lesson 23

a) 4 bars of PATTERN 3 SET-UP A.

b) 4 bars of PATTERN 3 SET-UP B.

c) 4 bars of PATTERN 3 SET-UP C.

d) 4 bars of PATTERN 3 SET-UP D.

e) 4 bars of PATTERN 3.

f) 4 bars of VARIATION 3A.

g) 4 bars of VARIATION 3B.

a) **PATTERN 3 SET-UP A:** Play this new ride cymbal pattern (the SHUFFLE PATTERN).

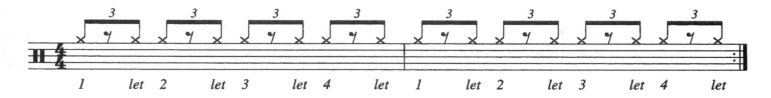

b) **PATTERN 3 SET-UP B:** Play the bass drum on all the quarter notes.

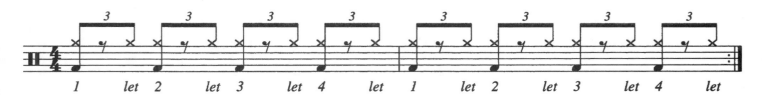

c) **PATTERN 3 SET-UP C:** Now add the SHUFFLE PATTERN on the snare drum. Since this pattern is identical to the ride cymbal pattern make sure the left and right hands line up evenly.

d) **PATTERN 3 SET-UP D:** Now play the left foot hi-hat in unison with the bass drum.

**e) PATTERN 3:** Accent (>) the snare on beats 2 and 4 with a rim shot.

**f) VARIATION 3A:** Play PATTERN 3 and add a crash cymbal on beat 1 of every two measures.

**g) VARIATION 3B:** Now play VARIATION 3A with the right hand on the hi-hat. In this pattern the left foot hi-hat is not played.

# HI-HAT GROOVE TECHNIQUES

## Lesson 24

### TECHNIQUE 1 (Hi-Hat on 2 and 4)

a) **TECHNIQUE 1 SET-UP A:** On beats 1 and 3 the heel is down while on beats 2 and 4 the toe is down. This technique will help you play 2 and 4 on the hi-hat. Play quarter notes on the bass drum while practicing this technique.

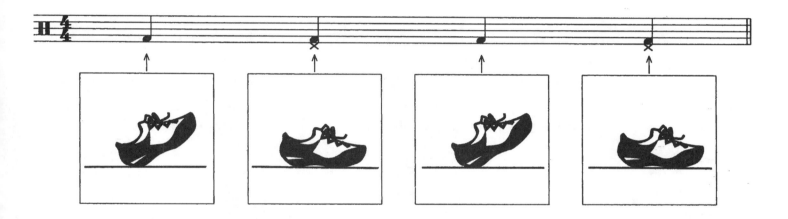

b) **TECHNIQUE 1 SET-UP B:** Add this ride cymbal pattern.

c) **TECHNIQUE 1 WITH PATTERN 1:** Now add the snare drum shuffle pattern.

**d)** ***TECHNIQUE 2 (Half Open - "Splashy Sound"):*** Ease up the pressure on the left foot so that the hi-hat cymbals are slightly touching. When the stick plays the hi-hat it creates the "open sound." An "o" above a hi-hat note symbolizes a half open hi-hat (Splashy Sound):

**e)** ***TECHNIQUE 3 (Left Foot Crash):*** Originally used to imitate the cymbal player in the New Orleans marching bands, this technique has become popular within the blues and jazz styles of drumming. With the ball of the foot on the foot plate (toe down) leave the hi-hat cymbals 1/4" open. Now slap your heel down on the foot plate to create a crashing sound. Practice this on all quarter notes of this pattern:

Practice these techniques until you are comfortable with each one, then go back and apply them to the various PATTERNS and VARIATIONS. It is important to continue practicing these techniques with all the patterns throughout this book. Experiment with different combinations until you find what works best for you.

# SHUFFLE TRANSITIONS (FILLS)

A way to move from one musical section to another is by playing fills. A fill should have the same consistency as the pattern you are playing. Like a pattern, a fill should never rush or slow down. To help practice all the fills in this book in time, first play them with the bass drum and hi-hat playing quarter notes. Then practice with the bass drum playing quarter notes and the hi-hat playing 2 and 4. Once you are comfortable with the time, take out the bass drum and the hi-hat completely.

Let's take a look at some popular blues fills.

## Lesson 25

a) 4 bars of SNARE FILL 1.

b) 4 bars of FILL 1.

a) **SNARE FILL 1:** Practice this fill on the snare drum.

b) **FILL 1:** When spread around the toms, the fill becomes much more exciting.

c) To help understand how a fill sets up a "musical transition," practice playing this combination (pay attention to how the music changes after the fill).

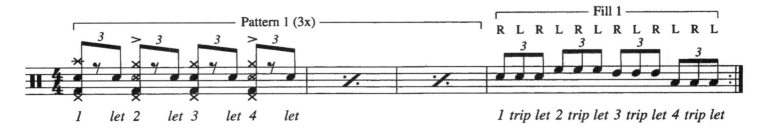

# *Lesson 26*

a) 4 bars of SNARE FILL 2.

b) 4 bars of FILL 2.

a) **SNARE FILL 2:** Practice this fill on just the snare drum.

b) **FILL 2:** When spread around the toms, the fill becomes much more exciting. Practice this fill.

c) To help understand how a fill sets up a "musical transition," practice playing this combination (pay attention to how the music changes after the fill).

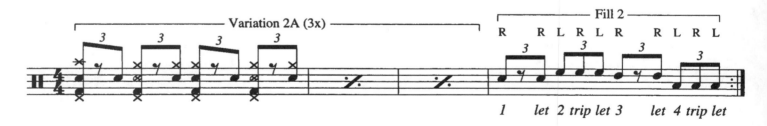

# *Lesson 27*

a) 4 bars of SNARE FILL 3.

b) 4 bars of FILL 3.

a) **SNARE FILL 3:** Practice this fill on just the snare drum.

b) **FILL 3:** When spread around the toms, the fill becomes much more exciting. Practice this fill.

c) To help understand how a fill sets up a "musical transition," practice playing this combination (pay attention to how the music changes after the fill).

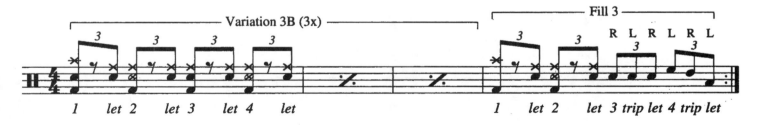

d) Now practice Lessons 25–27 with the music (minus drums). When you become comfortable with each one, try mixing all the patterns and fills in various combinations.

# DEVELOPING A SHUFFLE GROOVE WITH A BASS PLAYER

In this lesson, each major part of the **Shuffle Play Along I** (pages 58–59) is broken down into just drums and bass. Concentrate on locking in with the bass player and remember the triplet is the key to the shuffle feel.

## *Lesson 28*

### a) Intro

### b) Keyboard Solo

### c) Guitar Solo 1

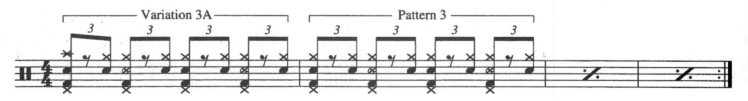

### d) Guitar Solo 2

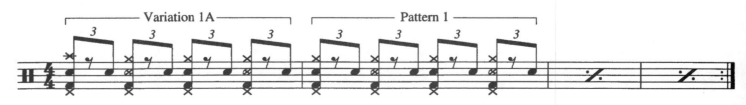

# SHUFFLE PLAY ALONG I

Follow the chart while listening to the **Shuffle Play Along I.** Pay close attention to the way each pattern corresponds with the music. Remember, in a shuffle it is important to keep the triplet feel throughout the arrangement. When you feel comfortable with the arrangement, go ahead and play along with the music with just a click.

♩ = 120

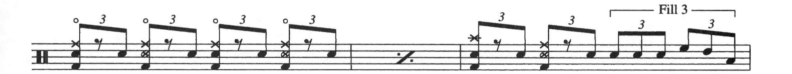

*Keyboard Solo:*

*Guitar Solo 1:*

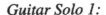

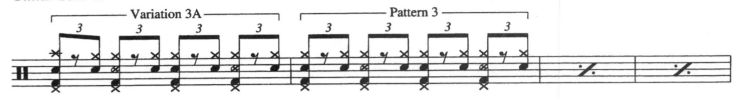

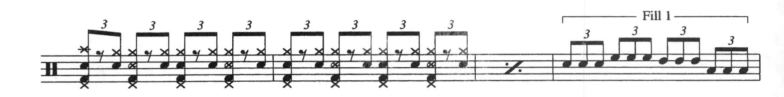

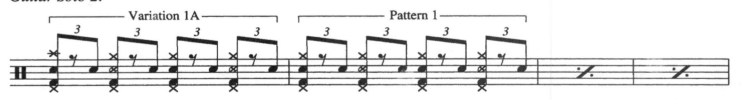

*Guitar Solo 2:*

# SLOW BLUES FEEL

## Lesson 29

a) 4 bars of PATTERN 4 SET-UP.

b) 4 bars of PATTERN 4.

c) 4 bars of VARIATION 4A.

d) 4 bars of VARIATION 4B.

a) **PATTERN 4 SET-UP:** Set this pattern up playing a steady triplet hi-hat figure with the right hand and quarter notes on the bass drum.

b) **PATTERN 4:** Now add the snare on beats 2 and 4.

c) **VARIATION 4A:** Play PATTERN 4 and add the crash cymbal on the first beat of every 2 bars.

d) **VARIATION 4B:** Now play VARIATION 4A with the right hand on the ride cymbal. At the same time, play the hi-hat on all quarter notes at first and then apply the 2 and 4 Technique.

## Lesson 30

a) 4 bars of PATTERN 5 SET-UP.

b) 4 bars of PATTERN 5.

c) 4 bars of VARIATION 5A.

d) 4 bars of VARIATION 5B.

a) **PATTERN 5 SET-UP:** Play the right hand triplet hi-hat with this new bass drum figure.

b) **PATTERN 5:** Now add the snare on beats 2 and 4.

c) **VARIATION 5A:** Play PATTERN 5 and add the crash cymbal on the first beat of every 2 bars.

d) **VARIATION 5B:** Now play VARIATION 5A with the right hand on the ride cymbal. Play the hi-hat on all quarter notes at first and then apply the 2 and 4 Technique.

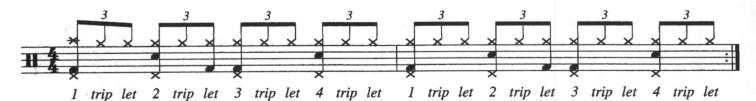

# Lesson 31

a) 4 bars of PATTERN 6 SET-UP.

b) 4 bars of PATTERN 6.

c) 4 bars of VARIATION 6A.

d) 4 bars of VARIATION 6B.

a) **PATTERN 6 SET-UP:** Using the same bass drum pattern from Lesson 30, add this new hi-hat pattern.

b) **PATTERN 6:** Then add the snare on beats 2 and 4.

c) **VARIATION 6A:** Play PATTERN 6 and add the crash cymbal on the first beat of every 2 bars.

d) **VARIATION 6B:** Now play VARIATION 6A with the right hand on the ride cymbal. Play the hi-hat on all quarter notes at first and then apply the 2 and 4 Technique.

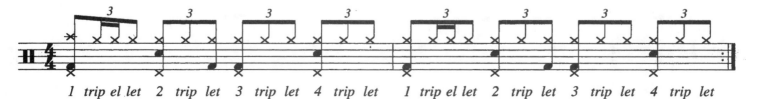

# SLOW BLUES TRANSITIONS (FILLS)

Remember when learning new fills to first play them with the bass drum and hi-hat playing quarter notes. Then practice with the bass drum playing quarter notes and the hi-hat playing 2 and 4. Once you are comfortable with the time, take out the bass drum and the hi-hat completely.

## Lesson 32

a) 4 bars of SNARE FILL 4.

b) 4 bars of FILL 4.

a) **SNARE FILL 4:** Practice this fill on just the snare drum.

b) **FILL 4:** When spread around the toms, the fill becomes much more exciting. Practice this fill.

c) To help understand how a fill sets up a "musical transition," practice playing this combination (pay attention to how the music changes after the fill).

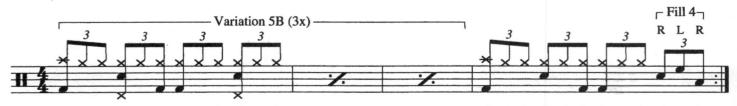

# Lesson 33

a) 4 bars of SNARE FILL 5.

b) 4 bars of FILL 5.

a) **SNARE FILL 5:** Practice this fill on just the snare drum.

b) **FILL 5:** When spread around the toms, the fill becomes much more exciting. Practice this fill.

c) To help understand how a fill sets up a "musical transition," practice playing this combination (pay attention to how the music changes after the fill).

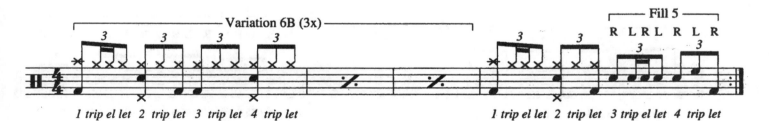

# Lesson 34

a) 4 bars of SNARE FILL 6.

b) 4 bars of FILL 6.

a) **SNARE FILL 6:** Practice this fill on just the snare drum.

b) **FILL 6:** When spread around the toms, the fill becomes much more exciting. Practice this fill.

c) To help understand how a fill sets up a "musical transition," practice playing this combination (pay attention to how the music changes after the fill).

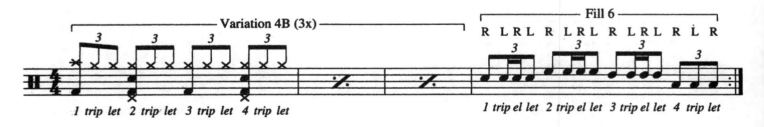

# Lesson 35

a) 4 bars of SNARE FILL 7.

b) 4 bars of FILL 7.

a) **SNARE FILL 7:** This fill begins at a low volume and gradually gets louder. This is shown in music with a symbol called a crecendo ( —————————— ).

b) **FILL 7:** Practice with both hands playing in unison (left hand on snare, right hand on floor tom).

c) To help understand how a fill sets up a "musical transition," practice playing this combination (pay attention to how the music changes after the fill). This fill also works well with the Shuffle Patterns.

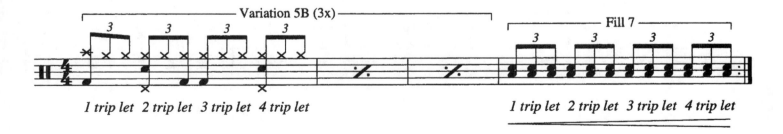

d) Now practice playing Lessons 32–35 with the music (without drums). When you become comfortable with each one, try mixing all the patterns and fills in various combinations. Do this until all possibilities are practiced.

# DEVELOPING A SLOW BLUES GROOVE WITH A BASS PLAYER

Look at each major part of the **Slow Blues Groove Play Along** (pages 68–69) broken down into just drums and bass. Concentrate on locking in with the bass player and remember the triplet is the key to the shuffle feel.

## *Lesson 36*

### a) Intro

### b) Guitar Solo 1

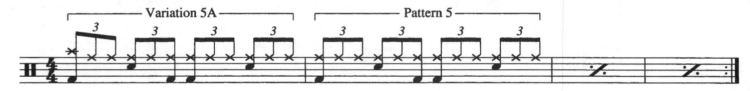

### c) Keyboard Solo

### d) Guitar Solo 2

# SLOW BLUES PLAY ALONG

Following the chart, listen to the **Slow Blues Play Along.** Pay close attention to the way each pattern corresponds with the music. Remember, in a shuffle it is important to keep the triplet feel throughout the arrangement. When you feel comfortable with the arrangement, go ahead and play along with the music with just a click.

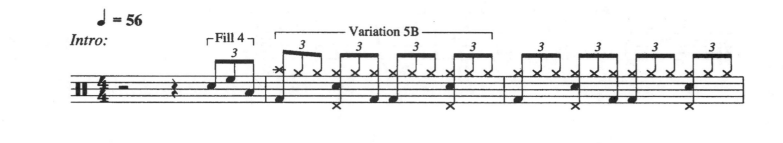

*Guitar Solo 1:*

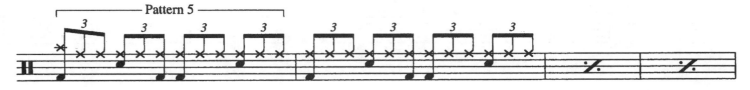

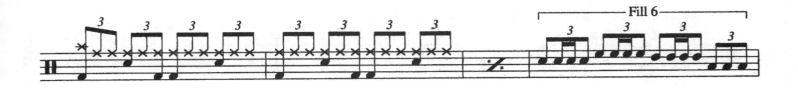

*Keyboard Solo:*

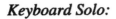

*Guitar Solo 2:*

# UNIQUE SHUFFLE STYLES
## *"The Charleston Feel"*

**Lesson 37**

a) 4 bars of PATTERN 7 SET-UP A.

b) 4 bars of PATTERN 7 SET-UP B.

c) 4 bars of PATTERN 7.

d) 4 bars of VARIATION 7A.

e) 4 bars of VARIATION 7B.

f) 4 bars of VARIATION 7C.

g) 4 bars of VARIATION 7D.

h) 4 bars of VARIATION 7E.

a) **PATTERN 7 SET-UP A:** Play the left hand shuffle pattern on the snare drum with this new bass drum figure.

b) **PATTERN 7 SET-UP B:** Play quarter notes with the left foot hi-hat.

c) **PATTERN 7:** Now play the ride cymbal on quarter notes in unison with the left foot hi-hat.

d) **VARIATION 7A:** Replace the ride cymbal part with the "jazz ride cymbal" (**Lesson 22** – pg. 48). Then apply the 2 and 4 Technique in the left foot.

e) **VARIATION 7B:** Replace the ride cymbal part with the "shuffle pattern" (*Lesson 3* – pg. 50) and continue playing the 2 and 4 Technique with the hi-hat foot.

f) **VARIATION 7C:** Play PATTERN 7 with the crash cymbal on the first beat of every 2 bars.

g) **VARIATION 7D:** Play VARIATION 7A with the crash cymbal on the first beat of every 2 bars.

h) **VARIATION 7E:** Play VARIATION 7B with the crash cymbal on the first beat of every 2 bars.

# "Steve Gadd Shuffle"

## Lesson 38

a) 4 bars of PATTERN 8 SET-UP A.

b) 4 bars of PATTERN 8 SET-UP B.

c) 4 bars of PATTERN 8.

e) 4 bars of VARIATION 8A.

f) 4 bars of VARIATION 8B.

a) **PATTERN 8 SET-UP A:** Play the bass drum on all the quarter notes and the left foot hi-hat on all the "let's."

b) **PATTERN 8 SET-UP B:** Now add the hi-hat in the right hand. Be careful not to make a "splashy sound" between the hi-hat foot and hand. Try to maintain the "chick" sound.

c) **PATTERN 8:** Add the snare drum on beats 2 and 4.

d) **HELPFUL HINT:** If you are having trouble playing this pattern, go back to SET-UP B (without the bass drum).

**e) VARIATION 8A:** Now play PATTERN 8 with the crash cymbal on the first beat of every two bars.

**f) VARIATION 8B:** Now play VARIATION 8A with the right hand on the ride cymbal.

**g) HELPFUL HINT:** If you are having trouble playing this variation, practice it without the bass drum. Slowly add it back in as you become more comfortable.

# UNIQUE SHUFFLE TRANSITIONS (FILLS)

These fills can be played with all the PATTERNS in this book. Remember to continue playing each new fill with the bass drum and hi-hat playing quarter notes first. Then practice with the bass drum playing quarter notes and the hi-hat playing 2 & 4. Once you are comfortable with the time, take out the bass drum and the hi-hat completely.

## "Quarter Note Triplets"

## Lesson 39

a) Using alternating strokes, practice triplets on the snare drum.

b) Now continue playing the triplets, but don't let your left hand touch the drum (put your left hand in the air — lightly shaded notes). What you hear your right hand playing are quarter note triplets.

c) In music notation, quarter note triplets are written like:

**d) SNARE FILL 8:** Practice the quarter note triplets between the snare drum and the crash cymbal. (If you have two crash cymbals, practice alternating the quarter note triplets between the two cymbals.)

**e) FILL 8:** Now play the bass drum in unison with the crash cymbal notes.

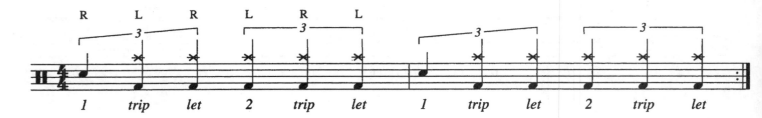

**f)** To help understand how a fill sets up a "musical transition," practice playing this combination (pay attention to how the music changes after the fill).

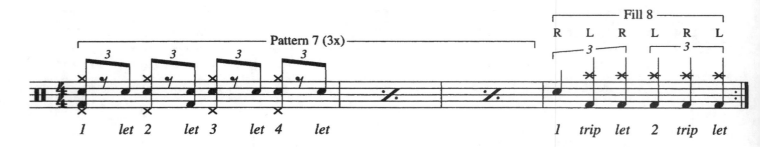

# Lesson 40

a) 4 bars of SNARE FILL 9.

b) 4 bars of FILL 9.

a) **SNARE FILL 9:** Practice this fill on just the snare drum.

b) **FILL 9:** When spread around the toms, the fill becomes much more exciting. Practice this fill.

c) To help understand how a fill sets up a "musical transition," practice playing this combination (pay attention to how the music changes after the fill).

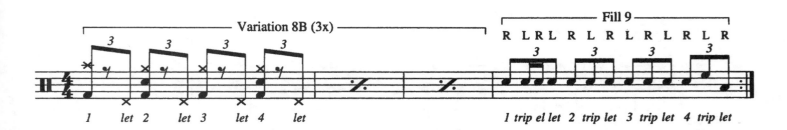

d) Now practice playing Lessons 39–40 with the music (minus drums). When you become comfortable with each one, try mixing all the patterns and fills in various combinations. Do this until all possibilities are practiced.

# DEVELOPING A GROOVE WITH A BASS PLAYER

## (using the Charleston Feel and Steve Gadd Shuffle)

In this lesson, each major part of the **Shuffle Play Along II** (pages 78–79) is broken down into just drums and bass. Remember to lock in with the bass player and keep solid time at the slower tempo.

## Lesson 41

### a) Guitar Solo 1

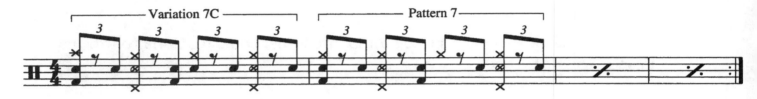

### b) Organ Solo

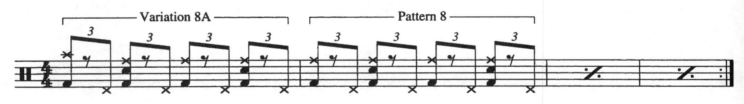

### c) Guitar Solo 2A

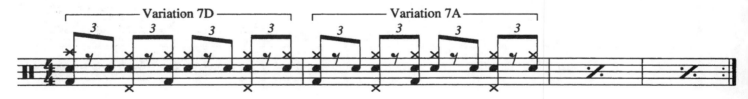

### d) Guitar Solo 2B

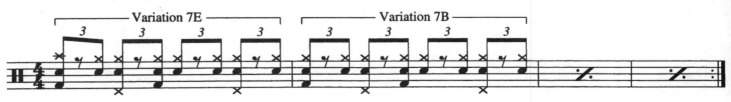

# SHUFFLE PLAY ALONG II
## (Using the Charleston Feel & the Steve Gadd Shuffle)

Follow the chart while listening to the **Shuffle Play Along II.** Pay close attention to the way each pattern corresponds with the music. When you feel comfortable with the arrangement, play along with the music without the drums. Remember to apply the proper groove techniques.

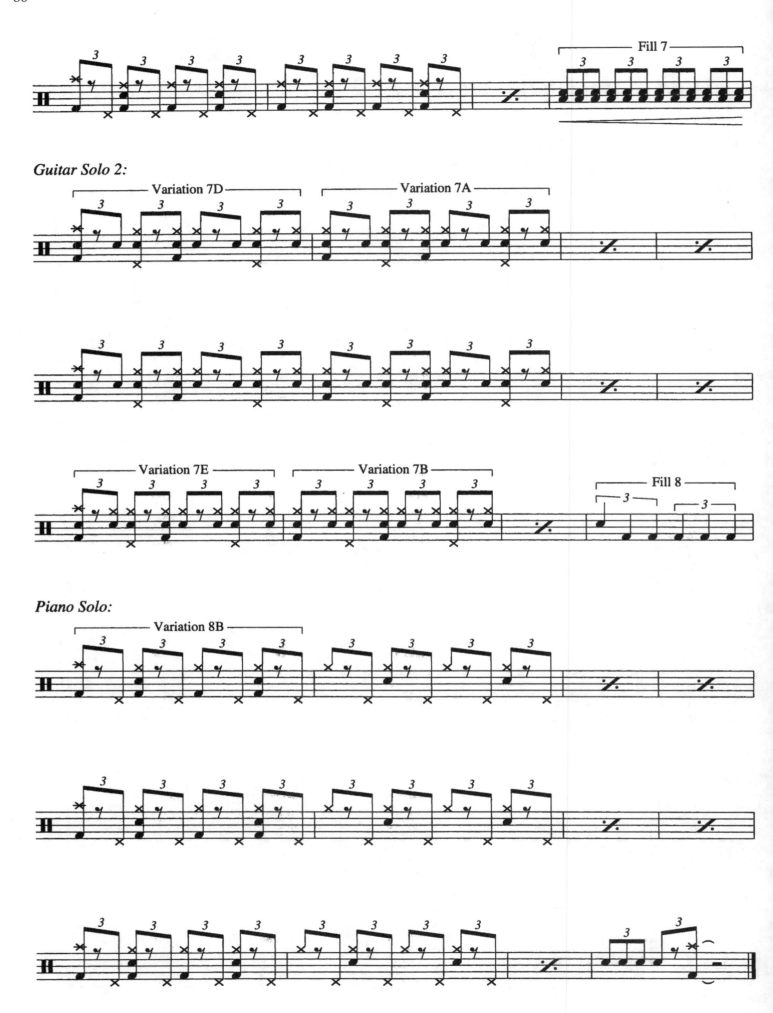

*Guitar Solo 2:*

*Piano Solo:*

# BLUES RHUMBA

## Lesson 42

a) 4 bars of PATTERN 9 SET-UP A.

b) 4 bars of PATTERN 9 SET-UP B.

c) 4 bars of PATTERN 9 SET-UP C.

d) 4 bars of PATTERN 9.

e) VARIATION 9A SET-UP.

f) VARIATION 9B SET-UP.

g) VARIATION 9.

a) **PATTERN 9 SET-UP A:** Play this pattern on the snare drum. Pay attention to sticking.

b) **PATTERN 9 SET-UP B:** Play crosssticks on the "&" of one and the "&" of two. To play a crosstick properly, place the butt of the left stick on the rim and the tip in the center of the head. Hold the stick with your thumb and index finger and place your palm on the head. You must experiment with the placement of the stick to find the spot on the drum that gives you the best sound (a sound similar to a woodblock is preferred).

c) **PATTERN 9 SET-UP C:** Continue by adding the tom on beats 4 &.

d) **PATTERN 9:** Now add this bass drum pattern with the hi-hat foot playing quarter notes. This is known as the Blues rhumba pattern.

82

**e) VARIATION 9 SET-UP A:** Play the Blues rhumba pattern with the right hand on the bell of the ride cymbal (⊘).

1 & a 2 & 3 & 4 & 1 & a 2 & 3 & 4 &

**f) VARIATION 9 SET-UP B:** Now add this bass drum part.

1 & a 2 & 3 & 4 & 1 & a 2 & 3 & 4 &

**g) VARIATION 9:** Add the hi-hat to complete this variation.

1 & a 2 & 3 & 4 & 1 & a 2 & 3 & 4 &

**h)** Practice both PATTERN 9 and VARIATION 9 using the 2 and 4 Hi-Hat Technique.

# BLUES RHUMBA TRANSITIONS (FILLS)

## *Lesson 43*

---

a) 4 bars of SNARE FILL 10.

b) 4 bars of FILL 10.

a) **SNARE FILL 10:** Practice this fill on just the snare drum.

b) **FILL 10:** When spread around the toms, the fill becomes much more exciting. Practice this fill.

c) To help understand how a fill sets up a "musical transition," listen to the example and then practice playing Fill 11 with the music (without drums) in this combination. When you become comfortable, try mixing and matching it with various patterns.

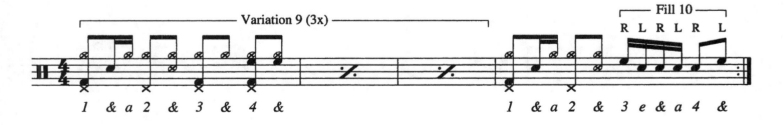

# DEVELOPING A BLUES RHUMBA GROOVE WITH A BASS PLAYER

In this lesson, each major part of the **Blues Rhumba Play Along** (pages 84–85) is broken down into just drums and bass. Remember to lock in with the bass player and keep solid time at the slower tempo.

## Lesson 44

### a) Guitar Solo 1

### b) Guitar Solo 2

### c) Guitar Solo 3

# BLUES RHUMBA PLAY ALONG

Following the chart listen to the **Blues Rhumba Play Along.** Pay close attention to the way each pattern corresponds with the music. When you feel comfortable with the arrangement, play along with the music without the drums. Remember to apply the proper groove techniques.

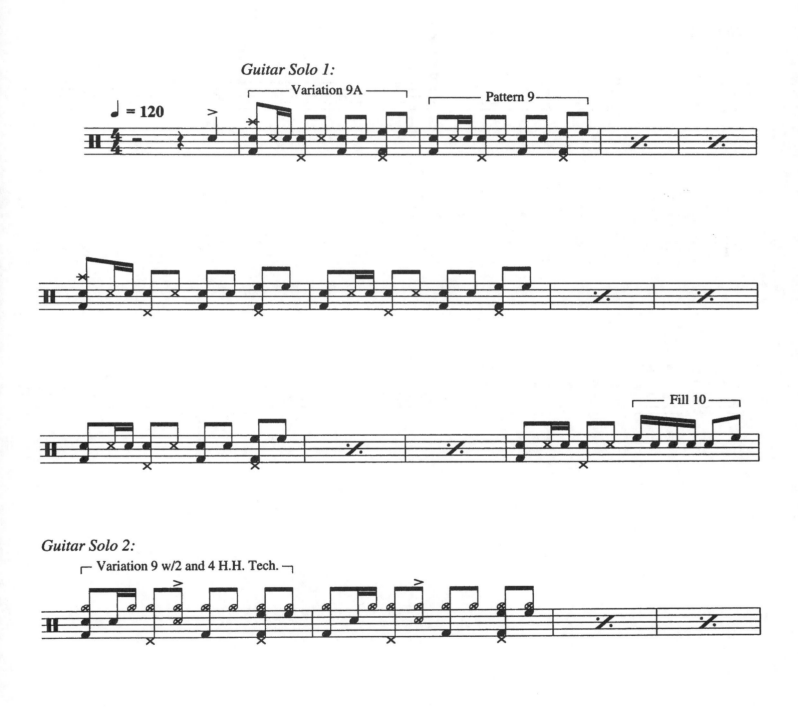

*Guitar Solo 3:*

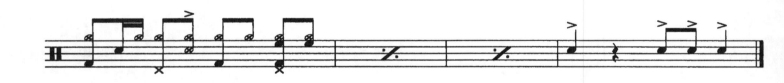

ROCK DRUMS

# BASIC ROCK PATTERNS
## (QUARTER NOTE BASS DRUM)

## Lesson 45

a) 4 bars of PATTERN 1 SET-UP.

b) 4 bars of PATTERN 1.

c) 4 bars of VARIATION 1A.

d) 4 bars of VARIATION 1B.

a) **PATTERN 1 SET-UP:** Play this pattern with the right hand and right foot only.

b) **PATTERN 1:** Then add the snare on beats two and four.

c) **VARIATION 1A:** Play PATTERN 1 and add the crash cymbal on the first beat of every 2 bars.

d) **VARIATION 1B:** Now play VARIATION 1A with the right hand on the ride cymbal and the hi-hat on beats two and four with your left foot.

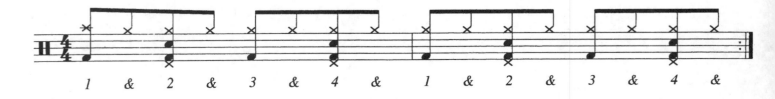

# Lesson 46

a) 4 bars of PATTERN 2 SET-UP.

b) 4 bars of PATTERN 2.

c) 4 bars of VARIATION 2A.

d) 4 bars of VARIATION 2B.

a) **PATTERN 2 SET-UP:** Play this pattern with the right hand and right foot only.

b) **PATTERN 2:** Then add the snare on beats two and four.

c) **VARIATION 2A:** Play PATTERN 2 and add the crash cymbal on the first beat of every 2 bars.

d) **VARIATION 2B:** Now play VARIATION 2A with the right hand on the ride cymbal and the hi-hat on beats two and four with your left foot.

# BASIC ROCK PATTERNS
## (EIGHTH NOTE BASS DRUM)

## Lesson 47

a) 4 bars of PATTERN 3 SET-UP.

b) 4 bars of PATTERN 3.

c) 4 bars of VARIATION 3A.

d) 4 bars of VARIATION 3B.

a) **PATTERN 3 SET-UP:** Play this pattern with the right hand and right foot only.

b) **PATTERN 3:** Then add the snare on beats two and four.

c) **VARIATION 3A:** Play PATTERN 3 and add the crash cymbal on the first beat of every 2 bars.

d) **VARIATION 3B:** Now play VARIATION 3A with the right hand on the ride cymbal and the hi-hat on beats two and four with your left foot.

# Lesson 48

a) 4 bars of PATTERN 4 SET-UP.

b) 4 bars of PATTERN 4.

c) 4 bars of VARIATION 4.

d) 4 bars of VARIATION 4.

### a) **PATTERN 4 SET-UP:** Play this pattern with the right hand and right foot only.

### b) **PATTERN 4:** Then add the snare on beats two and four.

### c) **VARIATION 4A:** Play PATTERN 4 and add the crash cymbal on the first beat of every 2 bars.

### d) **VARIATION 4B:** Now play VARIATION 4A with the right hand on the ride cymbal and the hi-hat on beats two and four with your left foot.

# Lesson 49

a) 4 bars of PATTERN 5 SET-UP.

b) 4 bars of PATTERN 5.

c) 4 bars of VARIATION 5A.

d) 4 bars of VARIATION 5B.

a) **PATTERN 5 SET-UP:** Play this pattern with the right hand and right foot only.

b) **PATTERN 5:** Then add the snare on beats two and four.

c) **VARIATION 5A:** Play PATTERN 5 and add the crash cymbal on the first beat of every 2 bars.

d) **VARIATION 5B:** Now play VARIATION 5A with the right hand on the ride cymbal and the hi-hat on beats two and four with your left foot.

# Lesson 50

a) 4 bars of PATTERN 6 SET-UP.

b) 4 bars of PATTERN 6.

c) 4 bars of VARIATION 6A.

d) 4 bars of VARIATION 6B.

a) **PATTERN 6 SET-UP:** Play this pattern with the right hand and right foot only.

b) **PATTERN 6:** Then add the snare on beats two and four.

c) **VARIATION 6A:** Play PATTERN 6 and add the crash cymbal on the first beat of every 2 bars.

d) **VARIATION 6B:** Now play VARIATION 6A with the right hand on the ride cymbal and the hi-hat on beats two and four with your left foot.

# BASIC ROCK PATTERNS
## (SIXTEENTH NOTE BASS DRUM)

## Lesson 51

a) 4 bars of PATTERN 7 SET-UP.

b) 4 bars of PATTERN 7.

c) 4 bars of VARIATION 7A.

d) 4 bars of VARIATION 7B.

a) **PATTERN 7 SET-UP:** Play this pattern with the right hand and right foot only.

b) **PATTERN 7:** Then add the snare on beats two and four.

c) **VARIATION 7A:** Play PATTERN 7 and add the crash cymbal on the first beat of every 2 bars.

d) **VARIATION 7B:** Now play VARIATION 7A with the right hand on the ride cymbal and the hi-hat on beats two and four with your left foot.

# Lesson 52

a) 4 bars of PATTERN 8 SET-UP.

b) 4 bars of PATTERN 8.

c) 4 bars of VARIATION 8A.

d) 4 bars of VARIATION 8B.

a) **PATTERN 8 SET-UP:** Play this pattern with the right hand and right foot only.

b) **PATTERN 8:** Then add the snare on beats two and four.

c) **VARIATION 8A:** Play PATTERN 8 and add the crash cymbal on the first beat of every 2 bars.

d) **VARIATION 8B:** Now play VARIATION 8A with the right hand on the ride cymbal and the hi-hat on beats two and four with your left foot.

# Lesson 53

a) 4 bars of PATTERN 9 SET-UP.

b) 4 bars of PATTERN 9.

c) 4 bars of VARIATION 9A.

d) 4 bars of VARIATION 9B.

a) **PATTERN 9 SET-UP:** Play this pattern with the right hand and right foot only.

b) **PATTERN 9:** Then add the snare on beats two and four.

c) **VARIATION 9A:** Play PATTERN 9 and add the crash cymbal on the first beat of every 2 bars.

d) **VARIATION 9B:** Now play VARIATION 9A with the right hand on the ride cymbal and the hi-hat on beats two and four with your left foot.

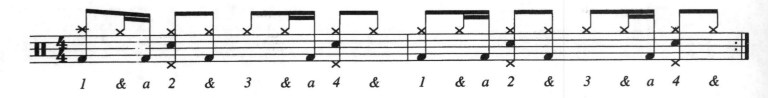

# TWO BAR PATTERNS

A musical phrase is a division of a melodic statement. Rhythmically a drummer can enhance this melodic statement by using more than a one bar pattern. PATTERNS 1 – 9, and their variations, were all one bar patterns. Now let's learn some two bar patterns and focus on how they change the feel of the music.

First listen to the difference between 2 one bar patterns vs. 1 two bar pattern.

## Lesson 54

The following two bar patterns are made up of one bar patterns you have already learned. Listen to each one and then practice them with a click.

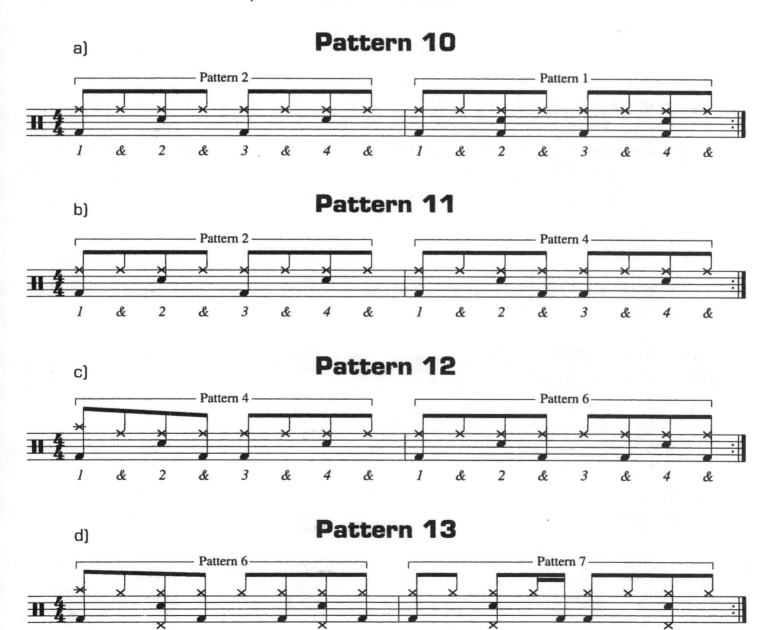

# ROCK TRANSITIONS (FILLS)

A way to move from one musical section to another is by playing fills. A fill should have the same consistency as the pattern you are playing. Like the pattern, a fill should never rush or slow down. When playing a drum fill it is sometimes helpful (and possibly musical) to play the bass drum on beats 1-2-3-4 and the hi-hat foot on beats 2 - 4. In each Fill Lesson, throughout the book, only the **SNARE FILLS** are notated this way. If you are having trouble keeping time when playing a fill, practice it with the bass drum / hi-hat pattern. Now let's take a look at some popular rock fills.

## *Lesson 55*

a) 4 bars of SNARE FILL 1.

b) 4 bars of FILL 1.

**SNARE FILL 1:** Practice this fill on just the snare drum.

**FILL 1:** When spread around the toms the fill becomes much more exciting. Practice this fill.

c) To help understand how a fill sets up a "musical transition", practice playing this combination (pay attention to how the music changes after the fill).

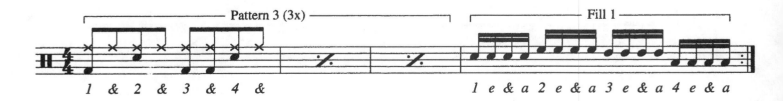

# Lesson 56

a) 4 bars of SNARE FILL 2.

b) 4 bars of FILL 2.

**SNARE FILL 2:** Practice this fill on just the snare drum.

**FILL 2:** When spread around the toms the fill becomes much more exciting. Practice this fill.

c) To help understand how a fill sets up a "musical transition", practice playing this combination (pay attention to how the music changes after the fill).

# *Lesson 57*

a) 4 bars of SNARE FILL 3.

b) 4 bars of FILL 3.

**SNARE FILL 3:** Practice this fill on just the snare drum.

**FILL 3:** When spread around the toms the fill becomes much more exciting. Practice this fill.

c) To help understand how a fill sets up a "musical transition", practice playing this combination (pay attention to how the music changes after the fill).

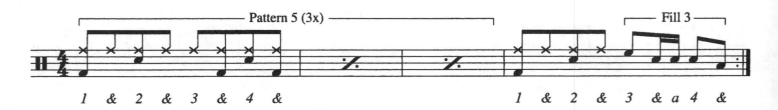

# Lesson 58

a) 4 bars of SNARE FILL 4.

b) 4 bars of FILL 4.

**SNARE FILL 4:** Practice this fill on just the snare drum.

**FILL 4:** When spread around the toms the fill becomes much more exciting. Practice this fill.

c) To help understand how a fill sets up a "musical transition", practice playing this combination (pay attention to how the music changes after the fill).

d) Now practice playing Lessons 55–58 with the music (without drums). When you become comfortable with each one, try mixing all the patterns and fills in various combinations. Do this until all the possibilities are practiced.

# ROCK GROOVE TECHNIQUES

Knowing many patterns and fills is the first step to making music. The next step is playing them with confidence. Play the pattern with an incredible feel and attitude. . . also known as grooving. Grooving takes a pattern and makes it sound and feel like music! Drummers who can groove are more than just drummers. . . they are musicians. A big part of a drummer's ability to groove is developed while practicing various groove techniques.

## *Hi-Hat Groove Techniques*

## Lesson 59 (Accented)

" > " is an accent mark. This symbol tells the player to play the note louder.

  a) 4 bars of Accented Hi-Hat Technique.

  b) 4 bars of Pattern 4 using Accented Hi-Hat Technique.

### a) **Accented Hi-Hat:**

### b) **Pattern 4 with Accented Hi-Hat**

## Lesson 60 (Half Open - "Splashy Sound")

Ease up the pressure on the left foot so that the hi-hat cymbals are slightly touching. When the stick plays the hi-hat it creates the "half open sound". An "ø" above a hi-hat note symbolizes a half open hi-hat (Splashy Sound).

  a) 4 bars of the Half Open Hi-Hat Technique.

  b) 4 bars of Pattern 4 using the Open Hi-Hat Technique.

### a) **Half Open Hi-Hat:**

### b) **Pattern 4 with Half Open Hi-Hat**

# Lesson 61 (Controlled Open)

The controlled open hi-hat technique is symbolized with a "o" to open the hi-hat and a "+" to close it.

    a) 4 bars of the Controlled Open Hi-Hat Technique.

    b) 4 bars of Pattern 4 using the Controlled Hi-Hat Technique.

### a) Controlled Hi-Hat:

### b) Pattern 4 with Controlled Open Hi-Hat

## *Ride Cymbal Groove Techniques*

# Lesson 62 (The Bell Accent)

When a "⊗" is used for the ride cymbal note, play the accent on the bell of the cymbal with the shaft of the stick.

    a) 4 bars of the Bell Accent Technique.

    b) 4 bars of Pattern 4 using the Bell Accent Technique.

### a) The Bell Accent Hi-Hat:

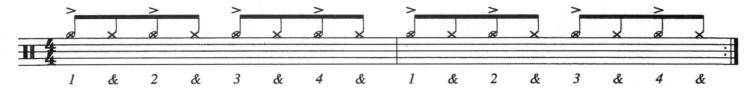

### b) Pattern 4 with the Bell Accent

## Lesson 63 (The Wash)

This technique is very common to rock drumming, however there is no musical symbol. It is up to the drummer to know when and when not to use this technique. This sound is created by playing the edge of the ride cymbal with the shaft of the stick. The overall effect is similar to the open hi-hat technique, but with a different feel.

    a) 4 bars of the Wash Technique.

    b) 4 bars of Pattern 4 using the Wash Technique

**a) The Wash:**

**b) Pattern 4 with the Wash:**

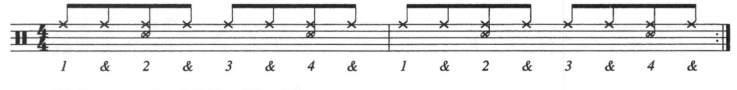

### Snare Drum Groove Technique

## Lesson 64 (Rim Shot)

A rim shot is created when the stick strikes the rim of the drum at the same time as the head. The symbol for a rim shot is " 𝄘 " in the snare drum space.

    a) 4 bars of the Rim Shot.

    b) 4 bars of Pattern 4 using the Rim Shot.

**a) Rim Shot:** Practice the right hand hi-hat pattern with the rim shot on beats 2 and 4.

**b) Pattern 4 with the Rim Shot**

Now practice *all* the patterns using the various Groove Techniques. Do this, with a click, until all patterns and groove combinations are practiced.

# DEVELOPING A ROCK GROOVE
# WITH A BASS PLAYER

Now that you have learned the fundamental groove techniques, it is important to establish the groove with the band. The first step is for the drummer and bass player to develop a strong foundation. In this lesson, each major part of the **Rock Play Along** (pages 104–105) is broken down into drums and bass. This will allow you to practice locking in with just the bass player.

## Lesson 65

a) Verse 1 (8 bars)

*Verse 1 & 2:*

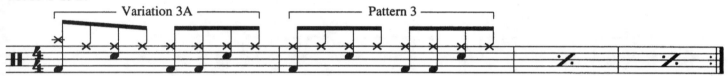

b) Chorus 1 (8 bars)

*Chorus 1:*

c) Bridge (8 bars)

*Bridge:*

d) Chorus 2 (8 bars)

*Chorus 2:*

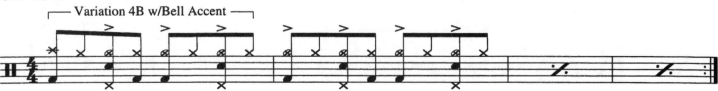

# ROCK PLAY ALONG

Now let's take everything you've learned up to this point and put it in a real song context. Follow the chart and listen to the **Rock Play Along**. Pay close attention to the way each pattern corresponds with the music and how the drums and bass work together. Also, listen to how the groove techniques are used to enhance the piece's musicality. Once you feel comfortable with the arrangement, play along with the music without the drums.

*Bridge:*

# THE ROCK BALLAD

A unique style within the rock format is the ballad. What makes it so unique is that it demands the characteristics of the rock style, but at slower tempos. A way to get used to these slower tempos, as always, is to practice with a click.

## Lesson 66

a) 4 bars of PATTERN 14 SET-UP.

b) 4 bars of PATTERN 14.

c) 4 bars of VARIATION 14A.

d) 4 bars of VARIATION 14B.

**a) PATTERN 14 SET-UP:** Play this pattern with the right hand and right foot only.

**b) PATTERN 14:** Then add the snare on beats two and four.

**c) VARIATION 14A:** Play PATTERN 14 and add the crash cymbal on the first beat of every 2 bars.

**d) VARIATION 14B:** Now play VARIATION 14A with the right hand on the ride cymbal and the hi-hat on beats two and four with your left foot.

# Lesson 67

a) 4 bars of PATTERN 15 SET-UP.

b) 4 bars of PATTERN 15.

c) 4 bars of VARIATION 15A.

d) 4 bars of VARIATION 15B.

a) **PATTERN 15 SET-UP:** Play this pattern with the right hand and right foot only.

b) **PATTERN 15:** Now add a crosstick on beats two and four. To play a crosstick properly, place the butt of the left stick on the rim and the tip in the center of the head. Hold the stick with your thumb and index finger and place your palm on the head. You must experiment with the placement of the stick to find the spot on the drum that gives you the best sound (a sound similar to a woodblock is preferred).

c) **VARIATION 15A:** Play PATTERN 15 and add the crash cymbal on the first beat of every 2 bars.

d) **VARIATION 15B:** Now play VARIATION 15A with the right hand on the ride cymbal and the hi-hat on beats two and four with your left foot.

# ROCK BALLAD TRANSITIONS (FILLS)

Let's take a look at some popular rock ballad fills.

## Lesson 68

a) 4 bars of SNARE FILL 5.

b) 4 bars of FILL 5.

**SNARE FILL 5:** This fill begins at a low volume and gradually gets louder. This is shown in music with a symbol called a crecendo. (———————————— )

**FILL 5:** Practice with both hands playing in unison (left hand on snare, right hand on floor tom)

c) To help understand how a fill sets up a "musical transition", practice playing this combination (pay attention to how the music changes after the fill).

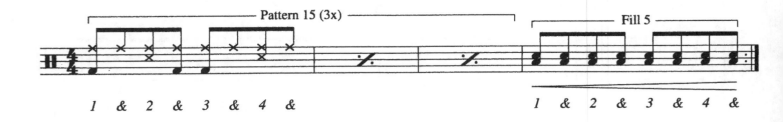

# Lesson 69

a) 4 bars of SNARE FILL 6.

b) 4 bars of FILL 6.

**SNARE FILL 6:** Practice this fill on just the snare drum.

**FILL 6:** When spread around the toms the fill becomes much more exciting. Practice this fill.

c) To help understand how a fill sets up a "musical transition", practice playing this combination (pay attention to how the music changes after the fill).

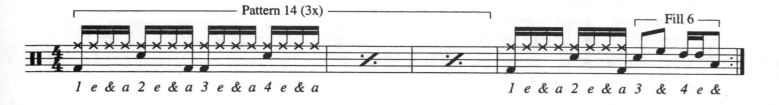

# Lesson 70

a) 4 bars of SNARE FILL 7.

b) 4 bars of FILL 7.

**SNARE FILL 7:** Practice this fill on just the snare drum.

**FILL 7:** When spread around the toms the fill becomes much more exciting. Practice this fill.

c) To help understand how a fill sets up a "musical transition", practice playing this combination (pay attention to how the music changes after the fill).

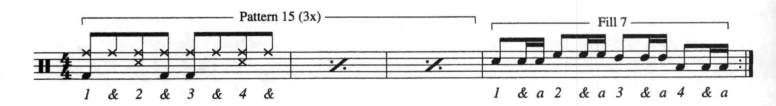

d) Now practice playing Lessons 68–70 with the music (without drums). When you become comfortable with each one, try mixing all the patterns and fills in various combinations. Do this until all possibilities are practiced.

# DEVELOPING A ROCK BALLAD GROOVE WITH A BASS PLAYER

In this lesson, each major part of the **Rock Ballad Play Along** (pages 112–113) is broken down into just drums and bass. Remember to lock in with the bass player and keep solid time at the slower tempo.

## Lesson 71

a) Verse 1 (8 bars)

b) Chorus 1 (8 bars)

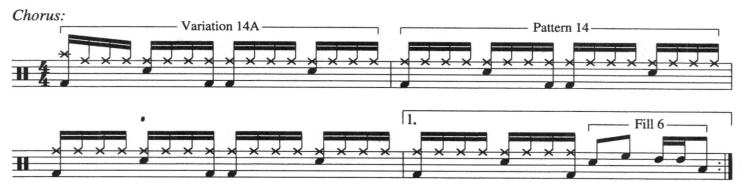

c) Solo (8 bars)

d) Bridge (8 bars)

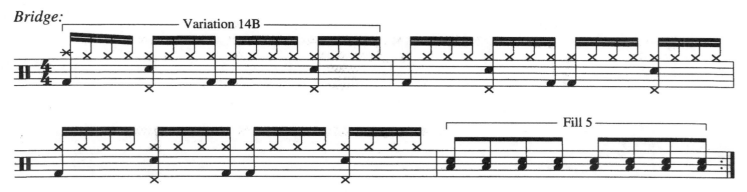

# ROCK BALLAD PLAY ALONG

Following the chart listen to the **Rock Ballad Play Along**. Pay close attention to the way each pattern corresponds with the music. When you feel comfortable with the arrangement play along with the music without the drums. Remember to apply the proper groove techniques.

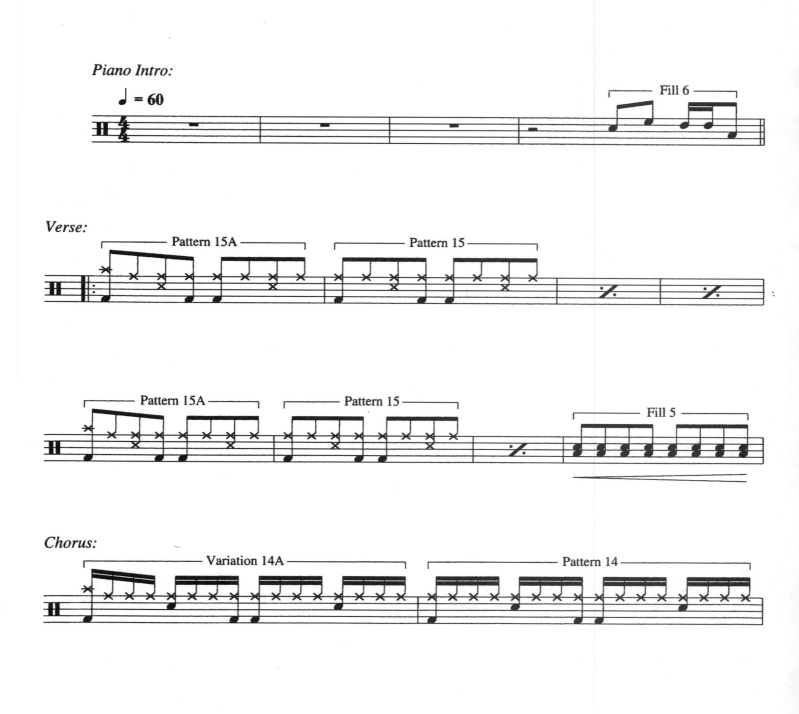

*Bridge:*

*Solo:*

*Chorus:*

# THE ROCK SHUFFLE

## *Lesson 72*

a) 4 bars of TRIPLET FEEL.

b) 4 bars of SHUFFLE HI-HAT.

c) 4 bars of PATTERN 16 SET-UP.

d) 4 bars of PATTERN 16.

a) **TRIPLET FEEL:** The rock shuffle is based on the triplet note value. A basic triplet pattern looks like this:

b) **SHUFFLE HI-HAT:** To create a shuffle feel, remove all the middle triplets. Practice this with just your right hand on the hi-hat.

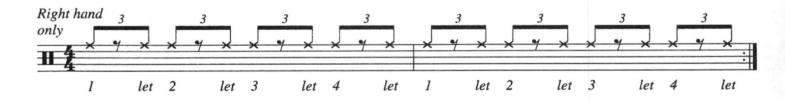

c) **PATTERN 16 SET-UP:** Now play the right hand shuffle with this bass drum pattern.

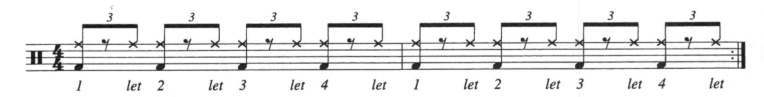

d) **PATTERN 16:** Add the snare drum on beats 2 and 4.

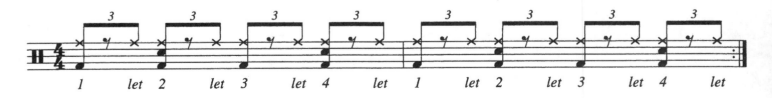

# Lesson 73

a) 4 bars of PATTERN 17 SET-UP.

b) 4 bars of PATTERN 17.

c) 4 bars of VARIATION 17A.

d) 4 bars of VARIATION 17B.

a) **PATTERN 17 SET-UP:** Play this pattern with the right hand and right foot only.

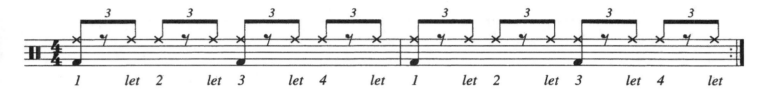

b) **PATTERN 17:** Then add the snare on beats two and four.

c) **VARIATION 17A:** Play PATTERN 17 and add the crash cymbal on the first beat of every 2 bars.

d) **VARIATION 17B:** Now play VARIATION 17A with the right hand on the ride cymbal and the hi-hat on beats two and four with your left foot.

# Lesson 74

a) 4 bars of PATTERN 18 SET-UP.

b) 4 bars of PATTERN 18.

c) 4 bars of VARIATION 18A.

d) 4 bars of VARIATION 18B.

a) **PATTERN 18 SET-UP:** Play this pattern with the right hand and right foot only.

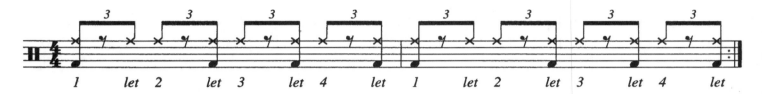

b) **PATTERN 18:** Then add the snare on beats two and four.

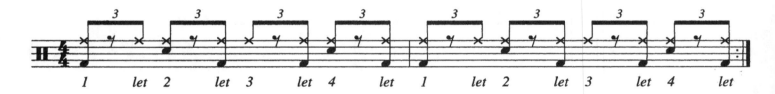

c) **VARIATION 18A:** Play PATTERN 18 and add the crash cymbal on the first beat of every 2 bars.

d) **VARIATION 18B:** Now play VARIATION 18A with the right hand on the ride cymbal and the hi-hat on beats two and four with your left foot.

# Lesson 75

a) 4 bars of PATTERN 19 SET-UP.

b) 4 bars of PATTERN 19.

c) 4 bars of VARIATION 19A.

d) 4 bars of VARIATION 19B.

a) **PATTERN 19 SET-UP:** A common rock approach to the shuffle is to play quarter notes with the right hand (using the half open/splashy hi-hat technique). Practice this pattern.

b) **PATTERN 19:** Then add the snare on beats two and four.

c) **VARIATION 19A:** Play PATTERN 19 and add the crash cymbal on the first beat of every 2 bars.

d) **VARIATION 19B:** Now play VARIATION 19A with the right hand on the bell of the ride cymbal and the hi-hat on beats two and four with your left foot.

# ROCK SHUFFLE TRANSITIONS (FILLS)

Let's take a look at some popular rock shuffle fills.

## Lesson 76

---

a) 4 bars of SNARE FILL 8.

b) 4 bars of FILL 8.

**SNARE FILL 8:** Practice this fill on just the snare drum.

**FILL 8:** When spread around the toms the fill becomes much more exciting. Practice this fill.

c) To help understand how a fill sets up a "musical transition", practice playing this combination (pay attention to how the music changes after the fill).

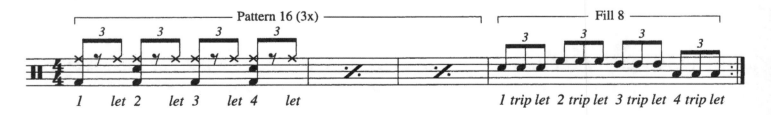

# Lesson 77

a) 4 bars of SNARE FILL 9.

b) 4 bars of FILL 9.

**SNARE FILL 9:** Practice this fill on just the snare drum.

**FILL 9:** When spread around the toms the fill becomes much more exciting. Practice this fill.

c) To help understand how a fill sets up a "musical transition", practice playing this combination (pay attention to how the music changes after the fill).

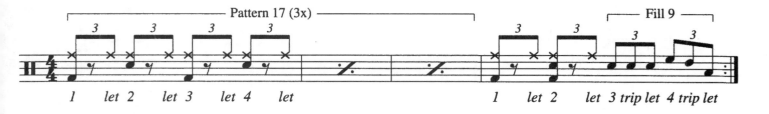

# Lesson 78

a) 4 bars of SNARE FILL 10.

b) 4 bars of FILL 10.

**SNARE FILL 10:** Practice this fill on just the snare drum.

*1 trip let 2    let 3 trip let 4    let 1 trip let 2    let 3 trip let 4    let*

**FILL 10:** When spread around the toms the fill becomes much more exciting. Practice this fill.

*1 trip let 2    let 3 trip let 4    let 1 trip let 2    let 3 trip let 4    let*

c) To help understand how a fill sets up a "musical transition", practice playing this combination (pay attention to how the music changes after the fill).

*1    let 2    let 3    let 4    let                          1 trip let 2    let 3 trip let 4    let*

# Lesson 79

a) 4 bars of SNARE FILL 11.

b) 4 bars of FILL 11.

**SNARE FILL 11:** Practice this fill on just the snare drum.

**FILL 11:** When spread around the toms the fill becomes much more exciting. Practice this fill.

c) To help understand how a fill sets up a "musical transition", practice playing this combination (pay attention to how the music changes after the fill).

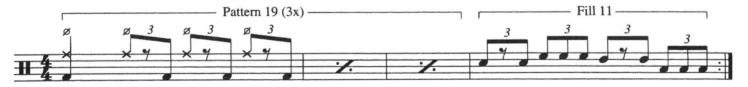

d) Now practice playing Lessons 76–79 with the music (without drums). When you become comfortable with each one, try mixing all the patterns and fills in various combinations. Do this until all possibilities are practiced.

# DEVELOPING A ROCK SHUFFLE GROOVE WITH A BASS PLAYER

Look at each major part of the **Rock Shuffle Play Along** (page 123–124) broken down into just drums and bass. Concentrate on locking in with the bass player and remember the triplet is the key to the shuffle feel. Since this play along is based on a 12 bar blues progression, each example is 12 bars with drums and 12 bars without.

## Lesson 80

### a) Verse (12 bars)

*Verse:*

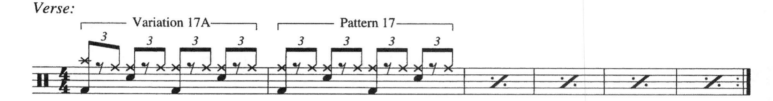

### b) Chorus 1 (12 bars)

*Chorus 1:*

### c) Solo (12 bars)

*Solo:*

### d) Chorus 3 (12 bars)

*Chorus 3:*

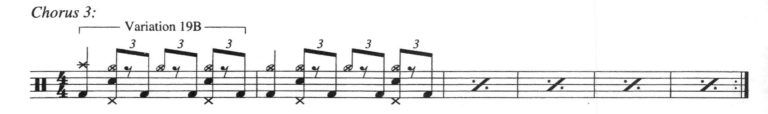

# ROCK SHUFFLE PLAY ALONG

Following the chart listen to the **Rock Shuffle Play Along**. Pay close attention to the way each pattern corresponds with the music. Remember, in a shuffle, it is important to keep the triplet feel throughout the arrangement. When you feel comfortable with the arrangement go ahead and play along with the music with just a click.

# HAND & FEET WARM-UPS
## (Note sticking for snare drum)